P9-CDL-935

No More "I'm Done!"

No More "I'm Done!"

Fostering Independent Writing in the Primary Grades

Jennifer Jacobson

Stenhouse Publishers

Portland, Maine

Stenhouse Publishers
www.stenhouse.com

Copyright © 2010 by Jennifer Jacobson

All rights reserved. No part of this publication may be reproduced or trans-
mitted in any form or by any means, electronic or mechanical, including photocopy, or any information storage and retrieval system, without permission
from the publisher.

Every effort has been made to contact copyright holders and students for permission to reproduce borrowed material. We regret any oversights that may
have occurred and will be pleased to rectify them in subsequent reprints of the
work.

Credits
Figure 2.6: "Editor's Checklist," from *The Big Book of Reproducible Graphic
    Organizers: 50 Great Templates to Help Kids Get More Out of Reading,
    Writing, Social Studies, and More* by Jennifer Jacobson and Dottie Raymer.
    Copyright © 1999. Reprinted with permission of Scholastic Professional
    Books, a division of Scholastic, Inc.
Figure 4.1, from *Andy Shane and the Very Bossy Dolores Starbuckle*. Text
    copyright © 2005 Jennifer Richard Jacobson. Illustrations copyright
    © 2005 Abby Carter. Reproduced by permission of the Publisher,
    Candlewick Press, Somerville, MA.
Figure 5.5: "Story Board," from *The Big Book of Reproducible Graphic
    Organizers: 50 Great Templates to Help Kids Get More Out of Reading,
    Writing, Social Studies, and More* by Jennifer Jacobson and Dottie Raymer.
    Copyright © 1999. Reprinted with permission of Scholastic Professional
    Books, a division of Scholastic, Inc.

Library of Congress Cataloging-in-Publication Data
Jacobson, Jennifer, 1958–
    No more "I'm done!" : fostering independent writing in the
primary grades / Jennifer Jacobson.
        p. cm.
    Includes bibliographical references and index.
    ISBN 978-1-57110-784-8 (alk. paper)
    1. Creative writing (Primary education) I. Title.
    LB1631.J34 2010
    372.62'3—dc22
                                                          2009042231

Cover, interior design, and typesetting by Martha Drury
Manufactured in the United States of America
PRINTED ON 30% PCW
RECYCLED PAPER

16 15 14 13 12 11 10   9 8 7 6 5 4 3

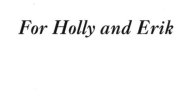

For Holly and Erik

Contents

Acknowledgments

This work represents more than twenty years of teaching writing, and therefore thanking all of the authors, colleagues, and children who have helped shaped it is quite impossible. I know that it doesn't take long for a brilliant idea to quickly become part of the collective thinking, and I thank all practitioners who have generously shared their inspiration and teaching techniques. Know that your observations, your attention to process, and your delight in the written word have had an amazing ripple effect. I've given credit when I knew the source.

Many thanks to Paula Flemming, my first instructor in writer's workshop. Through her guidance I was led to Don Graves, Jane Hansen, Peter Elbow, Nancie Atwell, Lucy Calkins, Ruth Culham, and Vicki Spandel, who have inspired me through their lectures and writings.

I also want to thank Mary Mindess at Lesley College and Eleanor Duckworth at Harvard Graduate School of Education—two of my professors who have never stopped whispering in my ear.

Special thanks go to Larry Frazier, Bonnie Reidman, and the teachers at William H. Rowe School who encouraged my early learning and discovery. Many of the practices developed in Yarmouth, Maine, are still a part of my teaching of writing today.

I am enormously grateful to Will Pidden, the principal of Durham Elementary School, both for his wisdom and for the opportunity to work with his staff for many years. Will not only has a tremendous understanding of teaching and learning, he also consistently applies this understanding to staff development.

Kudos, too, to the teachers at Durham Elementary who have kept up the writing dialogue, invited me into their classrooms, and shared their expertise. Many of those teachers are mentioned by name in this text.

Many teachers—from High Bridge, New Jersey, to Willits, California—have invited me to speak or conduct residencies in their schools. I almost always come away from these visits having grown in my own teaching and writing. Thank you.

I'm indebted to authors Nancy Werlin and Jane Kurtz, for their willingness to listen to me ponder while writing this text, and for offering valuable suggestions; and to Lori Jamison Rog, for sharing wonderful teaching ideas.

I am so proud to be a Stenhouse author! Bill Varner, my editor, was instrumental in helping me find the focus of this book, for which I am grateful. Thank you for your thoughtful guidance! And many thanks to Chris Downey, Jay Kilburn, Erin Trainer, Anne Sauvé, Nate Butler, and Rebecca Eaton, who carried this book from idea to successful fruition.

And finally, special thanks to two teachers—my first teachers—my parents.

Introduction

In 1986, I accepted a first-grade teaching position in Yarmouth, Maine. I was moving from private school to public and from an administrative position back to the classroom. I knew several things. I knew that I wanted, once again, to be working directly with young children. I knew, having been fired up by the work of Donald Graves, Lucy Calkins, Paula Flemming, and others who had piloted writing programs in nearby New Hampshire, that I wanted to establish a daily writer's workshop in my classroom. And I knew that I dreamed of becoming a children's writer.

I told my students on the first day of school that I was going to teach them everything I knew about writing, that I hoped they would teach me everything *they* knew about writing, and that together we'd all grow into the very best writers we could be. I no longer have my own classroom, but I'm still following the course I established on that September day. I embrace the dual identities of writer and teacher.

While trying to break into the children's field, I wrote magazine articles, textbook lessons, teacher resource books, and emergent readers for reading programs. Finally, years after setting my goal, I sold my first picture book. (And my aforementioned first graders? They were entering high school!) Since that sale, I have published many books for children—from beginning readers to young adult novels. I write, and I observe myself as writer.

As a literacy coach and author-in-residence, I continue to teach writing in the classroom. My students (including many fabulous teachers), teach me. We all grow in new directions.

This combined work has taken me down many wonderful paths of discovery but has in recent years come full circle to focus once again on the development of primary writers. How do we honor the varied developmental stages of our youngest students while teaching necessary skills? When is the appropriate time to introduce writing conventions? And perhaps most importantly (and what this book will aim to address most closely), how can we help primary students become independent writers?

No doubt the teaching of writing can be challenging at any grade, but particularly in the primary years when both skills and attention spans seem to be in short supply. Nevertheless, I've come to believe that primary teachers, with the very best of intentions, inadvertently train their students to be *dependent* rather than *independent* writers. Story starters or writing prompts, fill-in-the blank sentences or waiting until January to begin a writing program (when the students "know their letters") are just a few of the ways we communicate to students that they are not capable of writing and thinking on their own.

"Establishing a community of writers" is a phrase that has been overused, but I still promote the concept. I believe that in the most productive writing environments, the teacher and learner are one. Despite my high expectations for primary students and their ability to choose their own topics, identify and create organizational structures, and hone their language to meet the needs of their audience, I am always surprised by just how far young writers can go.

Two years ago, I was invited to do a weeklong author residency in Cupertino, California. The school is a public magnet school—parents are required to select and support its child-centered philosophy—but it has retained diversity on all fronts. I was in a first-grade room on my initial day, looking over students' shoulders as they wrote. My first glance at a journal frightened me. Edits covered the page: spelling corrections, cross-offs, arrows, insertions. I moved on to the next child and saw the same thing. I couldn't imagine in that moment how this heavy-handed teacher and I were going to join in our understanding of how children, or anyone for that matter, learn to write.

And then I watched something that astounded me. I watched a six-year-old boy, as he read his own work, pick up a pencil and cross off two whole sentences he had written. He wasn't being nudged by the teacher or a peer editor; he was making assessments about his own writing. The marks on all of these pages were not those of the teacher, but of the students. I learned a lot that week.

More commonly, when visiting classrooms I hear student comments along the lines of "How many sentences do I have to write?" or the premature "I'm done!" Both signal an unnecessary lack of independence and engagement in the writing process.

Teachers postpone student independence for a number of reasons. They claim children lack the necessary knowledge or language skills to write effectively, or that they're at the mercy of standards that require all students to demonstrate specific conventions by December. But I don't think these are the core problems. Supporting independence in writing means a slow but steady release of control—or of teaching practices that help us to believe we're in control. It means allowing students to be in different places: writing about different things at different times while using different materials. It means allowing our students to move through the writing process at their own pace and not in syncopation—never an easy thing to do when you have twenty or more active, curious, slapdash, impulsive students to teach. Nor is it easy to do when you're teaching something as complex as writing.

This book is an invitation for you to examine your own practices, both big and small, that foster independence in writing—especially for emergent writers. Guiding students toward independence takes time and a focus on the goal but is essential for the successful growth of writers at any age.

The book is organized chronologically, from setting up a classroom environment and establishing routines that foster independence to celebrating your students' initiative when they make important decisions around revision. You will find that this is not an offering of assorted ideas to pick and choose from, but a series of practices that build upon one another—each offering the basis for or an integral piece of what's to come. Therefore, I will not only try to present the benefits of each suggestion but also will explain what is lost if the idea is rejected so you may substitute or adapt the procedure to meet your own needs.

So turn the page and join me in the process of providing our youngest students with a vision of independence and, even more important, the desire and confidence to achieve it.

Chapter 1

Letting Go:
Teacher-Directed Writing
Versus Writer's Workshop

oday, Hannah has invited me into her classroom to observe her writing time. She bravely admits that this is her least favorite time of day. In fact she considers writing such a challenge, she often "lets it go," allowing something that feels more pressing to take its place. I love her honesty.

She reads aloud *Beast Feast* by Douglas Florian (1994) and pauses to point out lively, playful words. Then she stands and writes a prompt on the board: "Describe your pet." Anticipating the response of students without a pet, she quickly adds, "or a pet you wish you had." She asks the students to use words that create a picture.

As Hannah hands out lined paper, students at the first table engage her with questions and needs.

"Mrs. Mackie, Mason took my pencil."

"What if I had a cat, but it died?"

"Do we have to write the date on the paper?"

"I don't want *any* kind of pet," says a clearly decisive girl.

Hannah responds with the patience known only to primary school teachers and growers of extremely rare orchids. She resolves the pencil conflict, sensitively encourages the student to write about her deceased cat, reminds everyone in class to put the dates on their papers, and brainstorms an alternate prompt for the student who does not want any pet—though none of Hannah's other suggestions seem to satisfy the girl either.

Responses to questions and troubleshooting continue as Hannah moves around the room. Before she can reach the last table of students—kids who are having a lively conversation about who has the biggest muscle—she has stretched out the sounds of three words, reminded a student of the shape of the letter *h*, and dictated the spelling of *gerbil*.

There! Finally each and every student has a sheet of paper and all, for a few brief moments, are engaged with the task at hand. Hannah has two lovely conversations about the use of strong verbs, reminds one student to use his finger to mark spaces, and then the most dreaded words are uttered by a boy who received his paper first:

"I'm done!"

"Aidan," says Hannah rushing over to the boy, "Let me see!" She reads aloud: *I have a dog named Barney. He chews tennis balls.*

Hannah smiles. "My dog likes to chew balls, too. What does Barney look like?"

"He's black," says Aidan.

"And big!" says a helpful student working nearby.

"Write that!" says Hannah handing the paper back to Aidan.

It's her best strategy for extending writing time. But it's not highly successful. Hannah teaches first grade, and six-year-olds love to be *the best, the brightest*, but most of all—*the fastest*. As soon as one child says, "I'm done!" others follow in quick succession. The noise level rises and students cluster around Hannah to show her their products, but they gently wander off as she questions them—a kind of "No, thank you" to her attempts to get them to add more.

She looks up with me with a face that is clear to read. It says, *See why I avoid this?*

* * *

I often refer to this writing model as "Spinning the Plates." The teacher runs around trying to meet the individual needs of all students—getting the plates spinning, if you will—and then at the first "I'm done!" all the plates come crashing down.

So what's the alternative? A workshop model. I hesitate to use the terminology "writer's workshop" because it is one of those labels that has evolved to connote a wide range of often contradictory practices. In fact, Hannah may believe she is conducting a writer's workshop. But let's look at the difference between Hannah's writing time and Stacey's.

Stacey, who had lots of experience working with a writer's workshop model before moving to this district, quickly incorporates new ideas. She's used to having other practitioners in the classroom and eagerly welcomes another set of eyes (in the way we writers are always asking willing readers to provide feedback on our work). She begins her workshop with a mini-lesson on voice. She tells students she is going to write a story not once, but twice! She takes her marker and, on chart paper, writes a few sentences about her recent apple-picking excursion. Then she flips the chart paper and begins the story again, this time inserting words and details that reveal her unique feelings and perspective on the day. After reading both versions, she puts the marker down and asks, "Which of my stories has more voice?"

No doubt about it, the second story wins. Students are eager to point out places where Stacey's voice comes through in the second piece.

When the discussion ends, Stacey says, "Today, boys and girls, as you write, pay close attention to the quality details that show us who *you* are. Let your voice come through!" And then she asks, "Who knows what they're going to be working on?"

As students report briefly on their plans for this period, Stacey sends them off to the writing center. Each picks up his or her folder from the bin and selects a cup containing tools for writing and drawing. From there students settle around the room to reread yesterday's work, make additions or corrections, and write anew. Some students will begin new pieces, others will pick up where they left off the day before, and still others will use an editor's checklist to prepare their work for a writing conference. Many will choose to draw. For some, drawing is prewriting. For others, the drawing will be an integral part of their story.

A few students remain on the rug: two haven't formed a plan, one wishes to ask a question. Through brief questioning, Stacey guides the uncertain ones toward topics of their choice without resorting to "Why don't you tell me about _____" and confirms for the third student that yes, she is ready for a prepublication conference. The student nods and heads to the whiteboard to write her name under the heading "Editing Conference." She then gets her folder and begins working on a new piece. As Stacey stands, she flips on the classical music that signals "Quiet Ten." For ten whole minutes, the class will be silent, allowing everyone to settle into a space that is conducive to thinking, imagining, writing.

Stacey picks up her folder, sits down at the table, and writes.

When ten minutes have passed, she turns off the music and the first student signed up for a conference approaches. As the student arranges her work, both Stacey and I glance around the room.

The parent volunteer who comes in to publish student work has arrived and has welcomed an enthusiastic boy, who has prepared for this occasion, to sit next to her at the computer.

A girl in the corner is reading a story about her birthday aloud to another. She recognizes an awkward sentence and, picking up a pencil, stops to make it clearer.

Today's class leader has gone to the writing center, picked up a date stamp, and is circulating the room, asking: "Where would you like me to stamp your work?" Students point to the place where their writing began today.

Two students are belly-down in the science center. Inspired by a recent school performance, they have decided to work together on a play.

Stacey reminds the student who has come to confer that today they will be focusing on voice. After the student reads her piece, Stacey uses a predictable format of response: she reflects what she heard, points to what's working well, and then questions the budding writer to guide her to new understandings. By following this regular structure, Stacey supports her students' writing growth without overwhelming them (or getting behind by spending too much time with one student). Sometimes she ends a conference by sharing a writing tip or teaching one new skill. The student leaves the table eager to make improvements, but before doing so, she erases her name from the conference list to allow another student to sign up.

For the next thirty minutes the students prewrite, write, confer, revise, and edit while Stacey meets with as many individuals as time allows. One boy with "tired fingers" joins Stacey and her current conference partner at the table. Stacey welcomes him with a nod, allowing him to listen as she and the student talk about what makes good writing.

The big hand hits twelve, Stacey tells everyone that writer's workshop has come to an end, and the kids moan—just like they do at the end of every writing period. Nevertheless, they dutifully clean up their

Creates Dependence	Fosters Independence
Teacher selects writing prompt.	Students select writing topic.
Teacher is "keeper of supplies," handing out paper and pencils.	Materials are available in the writing center.
Teacher "stretches out" words or provides the spelling of words.	Students know that by "writing the sounds they hear" they are teaching themselves to read and write.
Because writing is assigned, students brainstorm whatever comes to mind in ten minutes and then exclaim, "I'm done!"	Students often plan what they will write in the future, and consequently organize their thoughts in the space between one writer's workshop and the next.
Writing lasts as long as a writing period or a journal page (or shorter!).	Students often work on the same writing piece for many days.
Students who are often minimally engaged in their work resist revision.	In anticipation of conferences, author's chair, or the possibility of coteaching a mini-lesson, students willingly revise.
All students publish their work at the same time.	Students publish on an individual basis when their work merits publication.

Figure 1.1
Creating
Dependence
Versus Fostering
Independence

writing supplies and move toward their cubbies to prepare for snack and recess. When they return to the classroom, they'll participate in a fifteen-minute "author's chair," where three students will share their work while others provide feedback.

In Stacey's class there is no such thing as being done.

So what's the difference between these two classes? Contrary to what one might think, there is no difference between the developmental stages, number of students who qualify for free lunch, reading levels, or distribution of students who are English language learners. These classrooms are across the hall from one another in the same school. Both teachers have high expectations for their students, but while Stacey has helped her students grow into independent thinkers and writers, Hannah, who is a truly admirable teacher in many ways, has inadvertently trained her students to depend on her. The table in Figure 1.1 lists just a few of the ways their practices compare.

By organizing the room well, presenting carefully crafted mini-lessons to teach students how to follow regular routines, and setting a tone that says, in essence, "We are all writers and all writing teachers," Stacey has fostered an independence that truly supports writing growth. Giving up control of the little things allows her to create an authentic, energetic writing time that keeps everyone productively engaged.

So where does one begin?

Chapter 2

Spaces That Support Independence

An optimum classroom environment can go a long way in helping young students work independently. Access to carefully considered materials and daily routines will build a strong foundation for your writing program.

I've seen writer's workshop work in classrooms the size of gymnasiums and in spaces no larger than a closet. Join me as I describe my ideal setting, which includes a meeting area, a conference area (optional in kindergarten), a writing center (not a place where students work, but a place where materials are kept), a good management system, and a publishing area.

Meeting Area

I choose a meeting area where I and my fellow writers will come together to discuss writing. When teaching mini-lessons, I prefer to have us huddled together on a rug rather than having students seated at tables or desks. The setting is more intimate and collegial, the topic at hand more timely. It's easy to maintain focus and allow students to

Many first-grade teachers complain of students lying down during meeting time. Believe it or not, there's a physical reason. Six-year-olds' shoulders are still developing muscle! Shoulders tire quickly and then the students go prone. This is a good reason to include time for moving around each day.

"pair and share" when they are sitting in a circle or a tight cluster.

Ideally, my meeting area is also my reading corner. Often during a mini-lesson, students will make connections to texts they have read. For example, while talking about the joy of refrains, a student recalls that *The Carrot Seed* by Ruth Krauss contains a repeating sentence. We reach for the book and sure enough, there is a refrain: "I'm afraid it won't come up," is expressed over and over again. We share the joy of excavating when we read from the actual book.

In addition to books, I recommend having in the meeting area a means of projecting sample writing and graphic organizers (overhead projector, LCD projector, or Smartboard) and a whiteboard or easel pad. Easel pads are great because you can look back on the writing, charts, or lists you and your class have recorded. You can also tear off sheets and hang them to use as a resources.

Conference Area

On my whiteboard is a permanent place for conference sign-ups. I have written "Conference" at the top and there are three spots to sign up below. Students sign up for conferences when they are inspired to share or when they would like to discuss any aspect of the writing process. They need not wait until they feel a piece is finished. Students erase their names after a conference, allowing other writers to volunteer. I conference with as many students as time will allow (names carry over to the next day).

Nearby is a table—ideally a round table—with several chairs. As any primary teacher will tell you, young students have a tendency to line up behind the teacher, eager to show their work. Partly to discourage this behavior, as it prevents me from conferencing with students who have signed up and keeps them from sharing their writing with peers, and partly to provide students who are overly active a positive place to light, I turn to the line and say rather authoritatively: "Sit down. Come on. You're welcome at this conference." Those students who had no intention of being pulled into listening quickly learn to read their work to a friend instead of lining up behind me. The students who do need a break from writing (such as the student in Stacey's room who had tired fingers) will usually happily join us, and I would rather have them attentive to writing instruction than disrupting classmates.

I keep a CD player within arm's reach. During the first ten minutes of writing (also known as "Quiet Ten," see page 8), I play classical music.

In the center of the conference table or nearby is my binder for keeping anecdotal records. I've tried many record-keeping systems, always hoping the next one will be more efficient and useful than the last. But of all the approaches I've tried, I recommend the use of a large three-ring binder. I fill it with notebook paper and use page dividers to give each student a section. For example, when Tomas comes to a conference, I simply flip open to his pages. I read my brief notes from our last session and then record what we discuss that day before I meet with the next student. This procedure adds continuity from one conference to the next. Additionally, in the front of this binder I keep a supply of sticky notes. I use the sticky notes to record what the child has decided to do next and adhere the note to his or her writing.

I should also point out that I use another type of record-keeping— one intended to keep track of how often students have come to conference, participated in author's chair (see Chapter 3, page 49), or published a piece. I want this information available at a glance, so for this purpose I use a traditional rank book or grade book. I record student names down the left-hand side of the page. The days of the week are listed at the top, and I use the following codes to keep track of events:

C = conferenced
P = published
S = shared work
T = taught a mini-lesson with me
A = absent

This book is not permanently stored at the conference table; instead, I carry it with me at all times and use additional codes to keep track of reading activities or the completion of a special project. Knowing what each student has done within any given week goes a long way in giving up the need to have every child doing the same thing at the same time—or giving students regularly assigned times to conference or publish.

Writing Center

For a time, I secretly feared that the real purpose of the writing center was to indulge my love of office supplies. (I'm drawn to Staples the way other women are to shoe stores.) However, as I've illustrated in Chapter 1, letting go of control of supplies helps your students behave independently and frees you to teach writing. After years of working in classrooms other than my own, I do believe having a supply center is essential to a well-oiled workshop.

The writing center (Figure 2.1) can be a permanent or mobile area in the classroom. I've seen writing materials rolled in on carts during writing time, or contained in shoe-pocket organizers that are prominently hung when needed.

Here are the supplies I store in my writing center. I've divided my list into two categories: items deemed mandatory and those that are optional.

Figure 2.1
The Writing
Center

Mandatory
- Writing folders
- Blank paper, story paper, notebook paper
- Date stamp and ink pad
- Pencils: standard and blue or green pencils for editing
- Alphabet charts (may be on folders or adhered to desks)
- Scissors and tape
- Graphic organizers
- Editor's checklists
- Scrap paper and supply request forms

Optional
- Stapler
- Pens (often preferred over pencils)
- Crayons, colored pencils, markers
- Sticky notes
- Baby name book
- Children's magazines
- Hole punch
- Brad fasteners

Let's look closely at the items and their purposes.

Folders and a Variety of Paper

Journals often work best for kindergarten students, because young children have such a difficult time keeping track of loose paper. Many first-grade teachers will wonder if they should provide journals for the same reason, but teaching students to manage loose paper in folders will allow for differentiation and encourage revision.

For first and second graders, I recommend using loose paper rather than journals. That's not to say that I don't use any journals: I love dialogue journals, response to literature journals, and learning logs. However, during writing time, I prefer students to be working with loose paper. Here's why:

The length of a piece of writing should not be determined by the duration of a writing period or by filling one journal page. Too often I hear kids say, "I'm done," when they've reached the bottom of a journal page.

Second, good revision techniques include cutting and taping, crossing out, and making substantial additions—all difficult to do when working with a journal. Journals are too often perceived as books, and most of us learn at a very early age not to "hurt" a book. Instead of pristine pages, we want to see examples of writers making important decisions around what to leave in and what to take out.

Finally, providing different types of paper allows us to meet the different developmental needs of our students. Though most of the children in a first-grade class are chronologically six years old (at least at the beginning of the year), you will likely see this developmental range:

Figure 2.2
Five- to five-and-a-half-year-olds prefer blank paper.

Developmentally five or five and a half: Students write with large letters, mostly caps. Rather than text moving left to right, it "wraps around" the page in no particular direction. Blank paper works best for children at this stage. (See Figure 2.2.)

Developmentally six or six and a half: Students are "slapdash," recording letters that are often sprawling and messy. The six-year-old appreciates story paper—paper that provides both solid and dotted lines to help keep letters to form. (See Figure 2.3.)

Developmentally seven: Students no longer want to write on large-lined paper, but beg to use the white paper with the narrower blue lines. Seven-year-olds are becoming increasingly focused, their letters grow smaller and more controlled, and they covet the paper that allows them to write more naturally. If you give a child who's developmentally seven blank paper, he or she will begin by drawing his or her own lines. (See Figure 2.4.)

Figure 2.3
Six-year-olds are happy with story paper.

Figure 2.4
Seven-year-olds
want smaller
spaces between
lines.

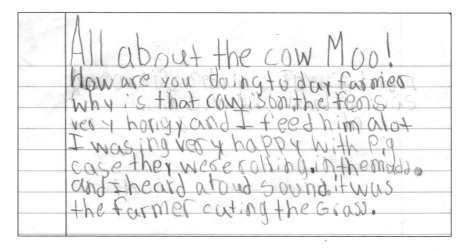

For writing folders, I use pocket-folders containing resources such as an alphabet chart and frequently used words laminated on the outside (Figure 2.5).

"But I provide alphabet cards on the wall," you might say. And true, someone—a very long time ago—decided that every primary classroom should have a trail of letters floating near the ceiling. There is something that feels so right about this long-held tradition, and yet for young students who work hard to recall the shape of letters and their corresponding sounds, this is not an optimum placement. In fact, it's a terrible placement.

Figure 2.5
Writing Folder

Think of the kindergartener who wishes to write the word *wagon*. First he stretches the word out: www-aaa-gon. He identifies the *w* sound, but does not remember the letter that represents the sound. So he looks up at the wall for help. Unfortunately, his ability to scan—to find the correct letter, memorize its shape, and then reproduce it on the page—is still fairly undeveloped. Often you will see young children try to "hold" the letter in their mind's eye, fail, and then have to relocate the letter on the wall all over again. In the meantime, two children who are preparing to leave the room for special assistance do catch his eye. He watches as they gather their things and wonders if he will ever be invited to participate in activities outside the classroom. They leave. He looks down. *What was he doing?*

One of the goals in the primary classroom is keeping our kids heads down! It is far easier to have the alphabet on the desk (either adhered or on a portable chart that can be picked up from the writing center) or laminated on the outside of the journal or writing folder. The more familiar your students are with the particular grid and symbols illustrated, the more they will use it as a resource.

In addition to laminating resources on the outside of the folder, I suggest students keep additional resources in the interior left-hand pockets. These might be lists of things they wish to write about, an editor's checklist, a completed story map.

Date Stamp and Ink Pad

The use of a date stamp does so much more than remind students to date their work. It provides me a way to monitor daily, individual writing progress, and it encourages students to move away from the idea that each new piece of writing begins and ends with one day's writing period.

"Date Stamp" is one of the weekly jobs in my writer's workshop. The student whose turn it is to carry out this responsibility goes to the writing center at the beginning of workshop time and changes the date stamp to match the calendar. Then he or she moves around the classroom asking, "Where would you like me to stamp your work?" Students point to the place on the page where they left off the day before. (Or they indicate the top of the page if they are beginning a new piece.)

This practice quickly helps students recognize that a single topic may be developed over many days. After a week or so of writer's workshop, a student will inevitably notice (and bring to everyone's attention) that the student sharing her work from the author's chair has "three date stamps!" Ah, this is admirable! Before long, many students move from writing brief, spontaneous snapshots to longer, richer pieces.

Date stamps also offer a concrete, visible form of accountability. I will question a student who has seemingly underproduced on any given day. Often a student will have a valid reason, such as, "I was publishing my snake story with Mrs. Olson," at which point I will say, "Of course! How could I have forgotten!" But in other instances I detect a pattern of avoidance and can focus my attention on the particular needs of that student.

Pencils and/or Pens

Most of us learned long ago that individual ownership of pencils does not work in the primary classroom. Therefore, desks or tables often contain a pencil cup or caddy. If this is your system, it is a fine one, though it is amazing how often students can still get in a tussle over who has the "best" pencil from the cup. You might try putting all of the pencils in the writing center, which gives students a larger pool to draw from and decreases their ability to determine which pencil has the most desirable qualities.

In addition to regular pencils, provide blue or green editing pencils —professional editors never use red, knowing that those little red marks wound the writer. Editing pencils help students focus on correcting conventions and encourage them to mark their paper as opposed to erasing (marks on a page demonstrate a writer's understanding and growth). But most of all, using an editing pencil simply feels quite grown up.

"But how can I stop my students from erasing in all stages of the writing process?" I am frequently asked by second-grade teachers. Although "the need to erase" can be a problem for some students at any grade level, it is a particular curse for second graders. Seven-year-olds are perfectionists; they want their writing to look *exactly right*. So they write, erase, write, erase. Much of the writing period can be taken up in this way. So what are we to do?

Remove the erasers from the pencils. That's right, snap them off.

Are you resisting this suggestion? Good! I want you to notice your resistance. You are probably thinking, "Well, there are some times when I do want my students to erase to produce a clean product."

Teachers are not responsible for creating this need to be perfect in second-graders—this is a mark of their development—but we do have to be careful that we don't give contradictory messages. In other words, we can't tell them that we don't want them to erase and then praise them for neat and tidy papers. The very best way to help a second grader release himself or herself from the tyranny of erasing is to praise the student for taking a different route: crossing off, adding a page of additions, drawing an arrow. These are the marks that make for a "perfect paper."

Another option would be to provide pens rather than pencils. Students love writing with the more grown-up ink, their work is easier to photocopy for a multitude of uses, and it eliminates the erasing problem altogether.

Scissors and Tape

"Spider legs" (page 46) and "surgery" (page 48) are two highly successful revision techniques readily employed by primary students, and both require access to scissors and tape.

I know that it's hard to imagine giving your young students free access to something as expensive as transparent tape. And yes, I also know that particularly in the kindergarten classroom, students will initially spend much of their workshop time cutting and taping and creating masterpieces that look nothing like any "book" you or I have ever seen. In fact, at this point in my explanation of what goes into the writing center, you may be convinced that I teach on another planet—or at least in school districts that are very different from yours. So let me address the issue of hoarding.

It is true that when students are first given access to the equivalent of a candy store for writing, they will often take more than their share. They will grab handfuls of paper, they will insist on trying every marker (especially if you, like me, adore the scented markers), they will break the tips of the editing pencils, and they will pull arm-lengths of tape off the roll. So why would you even think of making these supplies available?

Because after the first few days this behavior will stop. I promise.

Why does it stop? Because in addition to conducting a mini-lesson on the proper use and care of materials, you are beginning to focus not on the negative hoarding but on the amazing things some of the kids have begun to do with the materials. You will have Eli read from the wonderful book he created; you will have Nadine demonstrate the use of spider legs (which you taught her during a conference).

But mostly it stops because the novelty wears off.

And how do you prevent your entire (and perhaps very limited) budget of school supplies from being consumed in the first week? You offer your least expensive, almost-used-up supplies first. Instead of throwing out the broken crayons; the faded, tattered paper; and the nearly dry markers at the end of the year, use them to "open" your writing center. Think of it as recycling.

Graphic Organizers and Editor's Checklists

Graphic organizers are most successful when modeled for students first. Mini-lessons often include the completion of webs, story maps, or nonfiction planning sheets. When I'm sure students are familiar with a particular graphic organizer, I place copies in the writing center for individual use in prewriting and assessment.

Figure 2.6
Editor's Checklist
from *The Big Book
of Reproducible
Graphic Organizers*
(Scholastic, 1999)

Often the use of graphic organizers is optional; however, all students are required to store an editor's checklist (Figure 2.6) in their folders. After teaching or emphasizing a particular skill during a writing conference, I write it on the student's checklist. The student is then responsible for examining her writing to make sure she's applied her knowledge of that skill before participating in the next conference. Because primary writers are emerging writers, I keep their editor's checklists short. Often if a list has three items, and the student has begun to apply the skills regularly, I will suggest she replace her checklist with a clean copy from the writing center so we can start anew.

Scrap Paper and Supply Request Forms

Inevitably materials run out in the writing center and students feel the need to tell me *immediately*. While I'm conferencing, I

Figure 2.7
Supply
Requisition Form

Date:_____

Dear Supply Manager,

The _____ needs to be restocked in

the Writing Center.

Signed: _____

have a consistently enforced rule—one that I highly recommend. Students, barring an injury or major catastrophe, may only interrupt me with a note. In kindergarten and first grade, this buys me at least five more minutes of discussion, and the student who wished to interrupt accomplishes more writing. Second graders are quicker note writers, but less inclined to interrupt on the whole.

One of my first graders who *always* noticed when paper had run out but was loathe to take time from his own writing to write a long note designed a fill-in-the-blank supply requisition form! I ran with his idea and began duplicating a form (Figure 2.7) that was, as you can imagine, quite popular.

Optional Materials

The list of optional materials is fairly self-explanatory. The markers, crayons, and colored pencils are for prewriting, webbing, and illustrating. The brad fasteners and hole punch are for student-created books. The sticky notes can be used for sequencing events or information when prewriting, to make additions, to record questions to be addressed during a conference, or to record comments during a peer conference—and probably a myriad of other purposes. Two items that may need explanation are the baby name book and the children's magazines.

Let's begin with the baby name book. If you have ever asked your students to complete a story map before composing, you know that primary students have a tendency to fill in the *character* section with names of their friends. There's usually a lot of hubbub as students show one another what they've recorded. (Think Valentine's Day without the sugar.) This can be particularly disruptive in second grade, where the ups and downs of transitory friendships are often the undercurrent of the day, and feelings are easily hurt. But even if there was not a concern of social issues trumping writing, the main problem from a writing instructor's point of view is that fiction that features one's young friends quickly stalls after the introduction. Once students have listed the primary characters, the plot goes nowhere. Why? Well, for one, it's very hard for any writer to use his or her imagination when the material is real flesh and blood. And perhaps, once the fun of selecting and listing the characters is over, the story itself loses energy.

So I tell students that as an author, I never use names of people I know in my fiction. In fact, I do quite the opposite. I turn to a baby name book to find truly unique names—names that are seldom heard and will come alive on the page. (My first picture book, *A Net of Stars*, features Etta, Harper, and Fiona—names seldom heard where I live in the Northeast.) I place a baby name book in the writing center and suggest they try this technique. It quickly becomes one of my most dog-eared resources. (If you don't want to invest in a baby name book, bring in an outdated phone book, which provides first and last names.)

As for the children's magazines, I want children to become quite familiar with their formats and the various genres included in each issue. In *Ladybug*, for example, students can read stories, labeled pictures, poems, nonfiction entries, songs, rebus stories, and comics. The issues validate techniques young children use (labeling, for example) and model many types of writing to try.

I also refer to children's magazines when I introduce one form of publishing in my classroom: the Big Book. For the Big Book, I purchase a large, three-ring binder and a package of page protectors. Student pieces are often typed and printed on a single page. Writers illustrate their work around the edges—just like a magazine story. Students may read one another's work from the Big Book at any time, and if I have a few extra moments, I will open to where I left off last (a sticky note helps me remember) and read student work with much flair. I have even allowed students to "check out" the book and bring it home to share with their families. Placing a few sheets of notebook paper in the back allows for parents to write relished positive comments.

Management Systems

Directions for Creating the Monthly Best Writing Book

1. Staple six sheets of eighteen-by-twenty-four-inch construction paper together for each student
2. Write "Best Writing Book" on cover
3. Write the days of the month from September to June at the top of each interior page.
4. At the end of each month, use rubber cement to adhere writing—even stapled writing—to construction paper page. (Use rubber cement on the back side of the last page of writing—add a page if student has written on back side.)

In addition to setting up your classroom, you'll want to have a paper management system established.

For maintaining folders, I recommend creating a procedure that inspires you to clean them out once a month. As mentioned, my students store their work in pocket folders. Often they've stapled pages of writing together. At the end of each month, I sit down with individuals and ask, "Which of these is your best piece of writing?" This selection is then placed in the student's "Best Writing Book." (See sidebar for instructions.) I also share my opinion about which is the student's best piece of writing. When it comes to selecting the best piece of writing, sometimes the student and I disagree. I might choose the piece in which the student has used spaces between the words for the first time. The student might select the piece in which he wrote the word *underwear*, causing his classmates to fall down laughing during author's chair. The fact that we've chosen different pieces is wholly understandable. I am focused on writing development. The budding author is often focused on audience. Both of these areas are important, so both pieces will go into the best writing book.

I love the practice of ending each month with an evaluative conference, but I will warn you, these take time. Whereas I've learned to be quick and effective during my everyday writing conferences, my evaluative conferences stretch out like a humid July day. I always feel behind. So consider training another adult—an ed. tech or a parent volunteer—to help you with the best writing conferences.

What do I do with the remainder of student work? I chose one or two pieces to place in the student's portfolio and send the rest home. It's important that parents know that their students will be doing lots and lots of practice pieces throughout the year, and not every written product will be "corrected" or brought to publishing standards. Because I focus on the six traits of writing when teaching primary students, I will often have students write the trait we are focusing on at the top of the page (ideas, organization, voice, word choice, sentence

There are commercial stamps printed with the six traits. Students can stamp their work and then check the trait(s) they are giving special attention.

fluency, or conventions; these six traits were first established by the Northwest Regional Educational Lab in Oregon). This way, parents (with a little education during open house) can reinforce the effort that's exhibited in the practice pieces. To learn more about the six traits, see *Creating Young Writers: Using the Six Traits to Enrich Writing Process in Primary Classrooms* by Vicki Spandel (2007) or *6+1 Traits of Writing: The Complete Guide for the Primary Grades* by Ruth Culham (2005).

Publishing Area

Believe it or not, there was a time when primary schools established central "publishing houses." Students who had done an exceptionally fine job on a piece would be greeted by parent volunteers who typed up the stories and then carefully bound them into books. The books often had sturdy cardboard covers decorated with wallpaper samples, and pages carefully sewn with durable dental floss. The proud students would return to the classroom where they illustrated their books, which were later celebrated. Many books would find their way into the school library for the remainder of the year.

Very few schools still offer this model of publishing. Somewhere along the line, "publishing" came to mean "copying over your work without any mistakes." All students publish at the same time, removing the motivation to publish one's finest writing. Instead, students publish nearly identical teacher-directed products.

Here, I am going to suggest a publishing program that falls somewhere in the middle of these two models. Consider setting up an area in your room where you (or better yet, a parent or high school volunteer) can work with individual students. The volunteer sits at the computer, and the child sits next to the volunteer and reads his or her work. Volunteers (who you have trained) type the work using all of the proper conventions: punctuation, spelling, capitalization, proper grammar—keeping the child's original language whenever possible. If while reading, the student says, "Oh, I should have said . . ." The volunteer types what the child wished he or she had written, thus reinforcing revision right up to the end.

What do you do with the typed work? Here is a list of ideas:

1. Place in a class anthology (The "Big Book"; see page 23)
2. Mount on a bulletin board
3. Read over the intercom
4. Include in school or class newsletters
5. Post on a Web site
6. Have child read in a podcast
7. Record (audio or video) a class radio show
8. Perform as a skit
9. Read at an authors' tea
10. Compile a class book around a single theme (poems, funny stories, holiday stories, etc.)
11. Include in a class yearbook
12. Include in the school literary magazine
13. Submit to a student market or contest
14. Give as a gift

I do not recommend that primary students copy over their work. If we regularly ask student to rewrite, we are teaching them two things: write short and don't take risks. We also take away one of our best motivating tools. Being able to say something reinforcing such as, "Kara! You added so many quality details to this writing. Would you like to publish it?" goes a long way in motivating our students to be thoughtful, independent writers.

Chapter 3

Routines That Support Independence

Writer's workshop helps facilitate the following practices, which lead to significant student independence. Students:

- Write every single day
- Choose their own topics
- Receive differentiated instruction during writing conferences
- Examine writing to develop a vision of success
- Learn from mentor texts
- Focus on one or two goals at a time
- Benefit from the rewards of authentic audience
- Revise

If possible, provide a writing mini-lesson, writing time, and author's chair every day. In my first-grade classroom, I had a twenty-minute morning meeting (when I conducted a mini-lesson), twenty-five minutes for writing time, and fifteen minutes for author's chair. (Author's chair can be moved to a separate time if needed.) However, you can have a successful writer's workshop beginning with 10-10-10;

that is, a ten-minute mini-lesson, followed by ten minutes of writing time and then ten minutes of author's chair. I guarantee that once your class is successfully engaged in writer's workshop, you will insist on finding more time in your day for writing. And you'll know you've truly arrived when you gain an unexpected free moment and the kids shout, "Can we write?"

Mini-Lessons

"Mini-lesson" is one of those terms that has been in the educational vernacular long enough for us to feel it needs no explanation. But like most labels, it has begun to take on different meanings for different styles of teaching. So let me take a moment to explain what I mean when I talk of mini-lessons.

A mini-lesson is a focus lesson in which students are engaged in examining one quality of exemplary writing. Unlike traditional lessons, students are seldom asked to return to their seats and fill in a worksheet or complete an exercise that applies the lesson in isolation. (And we don't hear, "I'm done!" seven minutes later.) Instead, students return to their work in progress (or start a new piece if they don't have a work in progress) and try to apply what they've learned in the mini-lesson about good writing. Later, during conferences and author's chair, I will reinforce their attempts. I may even ask a student or two who have been particularly successful in applying a concept to teach the mini-lesson with me the next day.

Instead of thinking of lessons as a way to check off a curriculum requirement, know that each day you are planting seeds—seeds that will grow into a lifelong understanding of quality writing. Instead of mentioning a skill once, or for one week, you will return to these same concepts when appropriate throughout the year. In fact, your students will begin to take the lead in pointing out fine writing in all sorts of documents and especially in books you read aloud.

Every school has its own requirements and its own scheduling challenges, but I will share what works for me and for the many teachers I've been fortunate to collaborate with over the years.

My mini-lessons are part of my morning meeting, and like most morning meetings, mine follow the same predictable pattern. What may set my morning meetings apart from most is that I push up calendar and the math/counting activities that accompany the changing of the date to an afternoon meeting that occurs immediately after lunch. In other words, my morning is all about literacy (which integrates my social studies themes), and my afternoons are devoted to math and science. So how is my meeting organized?

I begin with a morning message. This is where I focus on conventions: phonics, capital letters, sentence structure, punctuation. Each day I ask, "What can you tell me about the print in this message?" Students take turns providing observations (which I circle or underline) and I, of course, gently guide them to the convention I most wanted to focus on that day. My messages are frequently stacked with digraphs, high-frequency words, question marks—whatever I think we need to take a closer look at next. The choices I make are directed by the students' readiness and an understanding of how young children come to understand print. (If you want to try teaching conventions in this manner but do not yet feel confident in sequencing phonemic elements, you might use a spelling textbook to help you determine which phoneme to focus on next.)

After morning message, I read a picture book—cover to cover without stopping—every day. Reading aloud is essential in every grade, but especially in the primary classroom. Not only do we need to provide students experience with texts, model reading strategies, and introduce new vocabulary, most of the qualities of fine writing—voice, word choice, sentence fluency, and (perhaps most surprisingly) organization—are best developed through reading aloud. Quite simply, the more you read to your students, the better writers they will become (see Figure 3.1).

I allow the first reading to be nothing more than a joyful experience. I want my students to fall into the rhythm of the text, to visualize descriptions and events, to feel the pacing of the story or presentation as the author intended it. The exception might be when I ask students to make predictions or raise questions—strategies that must be modeled before the text has been revealed.

However, I do not randomly choose books to read during this time. The book I select to be read aloud on Monday is the book I will use as a mentor text on Tuesday or later in the week. For my mini-lesson (which immediately follows my read aloud), I pull out the book we've previously read. For example, I might reach for *The Dirty Cowboy* and, as soon as the kids stop cheering, say, "Today I want us to look at the way author Amy Timberlake creates a movie in the mind of her readers." Why do the students cheer? Not only because *The*

Figure 3.1
Writing fluency
results from
listening to
literature.

Figure 3.1
Writing fluency
results from
listening to
literature.

Dirty Cowboy is a lively, humorous story, but also because, having now experienced the fun of this story together, it is, quite frankly, *theirs*. The connection they've established with this work—a sense of owner-ship you might say—creates a predisposition to feel positively toward and engage in the mini-lesson.

What I think often gets in our way of creating mini-lessons with confidence early on is a genuine understanding of and ability to articu-late what makes good writing—beyond conventions. Sure, we can dis-cuss the need for capital letters and periods with absolute authority, but voice or quality details . . . oh, that seems so much harder.

In this book, particularly in Chapters 4 and 5, I share many of my favorite mini-lessons for helping primary students grow into strong, independent writers. You will no doubt find many other mini-lessons presented in writing guides and online. But keep this in mind: mini-les-sons should have the tone of inquiry. Imagine you and your students are explorers of writing, and you won't go wrong. Don't have a mini-lesson for tomorrow? Go ahead and raise a question:

How do authors begin or end their stories?
How did the author organize this book?
How do authors make us want to turn the page?
In this story, what words jump off the page?

> Why do you think the author chose this topic?
> What do you think this author cares about?
> Does this story make you think of one of your own?

And then see what you discover.

In her book *Marvelous Minilessons for Teaching Beginning Writing, K–3*, Lori Jamison Rog (2007) provides a wonderful format for exploratory focus lessons. She creates a three-column chart and at the top writes: "Notice It, Name It, Try It." Students point out techniques or patterns they notice in the mentor text, they give the technique a name of their own invention, and then, as a group, they try to imitate the technique. Using the *The Night Is Singing* by Jacqueline Davies, students might notice that Davies asks questions in her poetry: "Sleep? Mama's feet?" They might name these "Quick Questions" and then try their own: "Hungry? Whose house?"

After the end of the mini-lesson, I'll often ask, "What are you working on today?" As students report, "I'm going to begin a how-to on skateboarding" or "I'm going to keep writing my story about the runaway truck," I send them off to the writing center to gather folders, additional paper, and any other materials they need.

Fostering Independence in the Selection of Writing Topics

Perhaps you're feeling skeptical at this moment. Perhaps at the end of a mini-lesson you've said to your students, "Today you may write about anything you wish," only to be faced with a class of bewildered, nonwriting students, protesting that they have no idea what to write about. Perhaps this experience has even led you to believe that your particular students simply don't have the experiences to draw from like primary kids in more affluent areas.

I will admit that students who spend an inordinate amount of time in front of television or playing computer games do present a particular problem. Their experiences are often of a virtual nature. (These are the same students who will have less success with prompts.) However, all children—no matter where they live or what their background—get the same 365 days a year. That's a lot of experiences.

I was teaching in a school in Lewiston, Maine, and a first-grade student wrote about the fence next to her apartment building. She explained that the police catch bad guys at the fence. Her neighbors blamed her daddy; they thought he was calling the police. But her daddy didn't need to call—the police just *knew* to catch bad guys there. Personally, I'd rather read a piece like this than one hundred personal narratives about trips to Disney World.

If you've been providing your students with prompts each day, then they are likely to have difficulty with choice at first. This is because choosing topics is a practice (and all the more reason for offering choice). In other words, the more we do it, the better at it we become. Throughout the year, I provide mini-lessons that give students new strategies for finding topics. Several of these mini-lessons are provided in the next chapter.

Does that mean that my students never feel stymied when it comes to finding an idea? No, writers do experience the occasional block. Often this simply requires a little time to think.

Thinking. Now that's something we have difficulty allowing in classrooms. Time after time I observe this scene. Students have gone to their desks. Josh is staring off into space. The teacher approaches and asks him what he's going to write about today. When he says he doesn't know yet, she provides him a prompt: Write about your favorite holiday. He's a bit sad because he had been hoping to come up with his own idea, and now he has to write about a holiday. And because he's seven, he worries about which holiday is *really* his favorite (seven-year-olds take words like *favorite* and *best* very seriously). Again he's left thinking. Now the teacher is annoyed, "Get going, Josh," she says, "or you'll have to stay in for recess."

Because school days have been compressed, because there is so little time to accomplish the long list of requirements, teachers want to see those pencils moving! But one of the very best forms of prewriting is *thinking*. I hate the question, "How long did it take you to write that book?" because I can't give an accurate answer. My latest middle-grade novel only took me six months to write, but that's because I'd been thinking about the story for the past ten years. And there are still rounds of revisions in its future. Our students can't take ten years to think, or even an entire writing period, but certainly we can give them the first ten minutes or so.

I was talking about this conundrum in a seminar recently when a parent came up to tell me her son's story. Her second grader was wondering what to write when his teacher approached him. They had the usual exchange, which resulted in the teacher saying, "I don't care if

Figure 3.2
A Second
Grader's Piece
About "Nothing"

> Christopher   #12   2/2/04
> Sometimes when you don't have
> anything to do you just do
> nothing. nothing nothing
> nothing. A really good place
> to do nothing is when you
> are in the car because besides
> looking out the window their
> is nothing to do. Another good
> place to do nothing is in the
> docters office becase unless
> you want to read magazines
> that are three years old you
> do not have anything to do.
> but you can never really be
> doing nothing because you are
> thinking so you are still doing
>   something

you write about nothing, get going." Figure 3.2 shows what that student wrote.

Now, I actually think Figure 3.2 shows a brilliant piece. And in fact, it's a story that contradicts my philosophy. The teacher, in a sense, provided the topic and the child ran with it, producing something wholly unique. But here is the sad ending: The boy was reprimanded for disrespect, and Mom was called into school to discuss the way in which her son had mocked the teacher.

Even the most well-meaning teachers (teachers who wouldn't say, "I don't care" because we do care) can fall into the lengthy, "I don't know what to write about," chat. It usually goes like this:

Teacher: What are you going to write about today?
Student: (*Shrugs.*)
Teacher: What did you do over the weekend?
Student: (*Shrugs.*)
Teacher: Did you stay at home?
Student: We went to Chuck E. Cheese.
Teacher: I've never been to Chuck E. Cheese! Would you like to
     write about that?
Student: (*Shakes her head no.*)

You know the trap! The student doesn't mind if this conversation goes on indefinitely, and here are two reasons why: she has your undivided attention and she doesn't have to begin (beginning is often the hard part).

That's not to say, of course, that students don't get stuck from time to time in thinking up topics—we all do. So how can you help?

First of all, refrain from circling around the room. You will be hooked into helping students who may have quite naturally done some thinking and then confidently begun. Instead, remain in your meeting area. Ask the question: "What will you work on today?" and allow those students who have a clear idea to leave the meeting area and get started. Keep those students who are unsure seated on the rug. Now you can have a conversation with this small group, which often leads students to inspiration. However, if a student still hasn't come up with a topic, you might say, "Okay, feel free to stay on the rug until you've thought of something. I know you can," and head to your table to write, thus shifting the responsibility to the student, where it belongs.

If your students write regularly, if you allow students to choose their topics most of the time, if you conduct daily conferences and author's chair, thinking will happen not just at the beginning of writing time. It will happen throughout the day. For example, a child will invent a game on the playground and think to herself, "That's what I'm going to write about tomorrow." As the day goes on, she'll recall details of the game she plans to include in

 Reading aloud books about everyday experiences will often spark student's own stories. Here are some particularly successful titles:

The Hello, Goodbye Window by Norton Juster (2005). A child visits her grandparents.
Pictures from Our Vacation by Lynne Rae Perkins (2007). Children go on a low-key vacation to a family farm.
I Lost My Tooth in Africa by Penda Diakite (2006). A child in loses a tooth in Mali.
Traction Man Is Here! by Mini Grey (2005). A Child receives an action figure in the mail. This story celebrates pretend play.
The Snowy Day by Ezra Jack Keats (1962). A child goes outside to play in the snow.

her piece—and when she does sit down to write, the piece will be surprisingly well sequenced. Or she will listen to a classmate's story about losing a tooth and think, "Oh, I have a funny loose tooth story. That's what I'm going to write about next!" Before long your students will queue up their stories. They will resist the urge to tell you things that are occurring in their lives, knowing that if they write about them, you will give them your undivided attention during a writing conference.

Occasionally a teacher will object to having students choose their own topics. "After all," she or he will say, "our kids are tested with writing prompts and need to be prepared." I understand the logic, which goes something like this: "Since our students are assessed with prompts, I'll give them a prompt every single day and when they're tested this spring, they will be pros." And it would make good sense, except that it's very hard to find intrinsic motivation to grow as a writer when given a series of arbitrary, inauthentic writing assignments. When students ask, "How many sentences does it have to be?" we know they are not aspiring to do the best writing they can.

Additionally, writing prompts tend to inspire lists. Why? Because they ask students to write on demand. When students have ten minutes to write on a topic they have just been presented with, they tend to brainstorm on the paper, writing everything that comes to mind. As a result, these pieces often lack organization or quality details. Once students are used to "blurting" during writing time, it's hard to break them of this pattern.

And finally, writing often conveys strong voice when there is enthusiasm for one's topic. When students care about what they write, they bring an energy to the writing—and details that convey a unique perspective. A prompt may or may not interest a student, and the quality of writing will reflect this. Imagine, at this moment, being asked to write a personal narrative on your special place. Perhaps you have a special place and you can't wait to share your fond memories. Or perhaps no place comes to mind as being particularly special. If this is the case, the writing of each sentence is going to feel like riding a tricycle through molasses (to paraphrase Orson Welles). Pure drudgery.

The problem with so many prompts is that the adults who thought them up (and I confess that as a freelancer I have written writing prompts) have never tried them. We ask students to write about the first time they did something and then we groan when every single piece begins with "The first time I ever . . ."

So instead, inspire your students to write from the heart day after day *and then* teach them how to apply what they know to writing prompts. Teach them to take a prompt and focus the topic to the personal. For example, if the prompt asks students to write about their favorite holiday, suggest they not write about trick or treating ("On Halloween, we get dressed up and go trick or treating. I get lots of candy. Halloween is fun.") but instead write about the year they dressed up as cuckoo clock and marched in the school parade, or the year they dropped their candy bag but their big brother stopped to help gather the candy up. Remind them to use their skill in using quality details—a skill they've been happy to hone as they wrote about things that really mattered.

What to do with all those story starter kits you purchased for your classroom? Place them in your writing center. When blocked, students can look through them to see if anything sparks their imagination. This is very different than being told what to write every day.

And now that I've gone on about the importance of providing students with choice (and it's essential for independence), I will say that occasionally I do want everyone in my class to try something—a writing exercise, if you will, that will build a specific set of writing muscles. For example, I might ask that students write three different beginnings for a piece—using three different author strategies. Or I might ask that students revisit their work from the day before and circle any action words that could be replaced with more vivid verbs. I call these days "have-to days," though teacher Bobbi Maunsell calls them "must-do days," and I have to admit the writer in me prefers the sound of that. So occasionally I will say something such as, "I know you are all working on pieces you love, but before you return to that work today, I would like you to try . . ." and I will give a brief assignment. Students know that when they've completed my request, they can jump right back into the writing they planned to do.

Writing Time

Now I've moved from the meeting area to the conference table, and Quiet Ten has begun. I turn on the classical music and write. I know that this is extremely hard to do. You have trained your students to work quietly for ten whole minutes, and the temptation to call in the lunch count or to correct last night's homework is bearing down on you. Don't give in. Know that writing alongside your students is the very thing that will have the greatest effect on their writing growth. Why? First, you are demonstrating your commitment to writing as an important means of communication. Children have always wanted to emulate the activities of adults (especially the adults they adore) and so will happily write when you're writing. Second, when you write, you gradually shift from being the writing teacher to a writing colleague. If a student approaches you and says, "I don't know how to end this," you find yourself saying, "You know, I have difficulty ending pieces, too. But you know what I did yesterday? I went into the reading corner and read the endings to several picture books and then suddenly I knew what I wanted to do." You are now an insider to the writing process, and your responses to students are not only more authentic, they are more helpful.

Refrain from talking to students during Quiet Ten. If you do talk, even in whispers, your students will, too. And the music, if heard, will act as a trigger. Let me explain.

Most professional writers will confess to using prewriting rituals. Some light a candle, or utter a sequence of words. Some sharpen number two pencils, peel an orange, or fix themselves a cup of licorice tea. For years, I would turn on a Native American drumming tape. Although this must sound rather "witty," as a friend of mine would say, the reasons these rituals work can probably be easily explained. Pavlov would call the ritual a conditioned stimulus; the writer's reaction, the conditioned response. Quite simply, our brains respond to a predictable stimulus by giving us a desired behavior: the urge to write.

Jessica DeJongh, then a first- and second-grade multiage teacher, told me a story I enjoy sharing. She was out one day and left her substitute detailed instructions. At the onset of writing time, the substitute teacher turned on Pachelbel's Canon and watched her charges dive into writing. "Wow!" she thought. The music worked beautifully. That afternoon, after giving the students a math task, she turned the CD on again. The students could not focus: they flitted around the room, talked, and genuinely ignored the math work at hand. The substitute said, "What happened? You were so good this morning!" And the students responded: "We feel like writing!"

Because I want the music to act as a trigger, I don't play it throughout writing time. I turn it off after ten minutes and allow the murmur of collaboration to occur. Most students, now deeply engaged in their work, will go right on writing. But a few will be ready to read their

Figure 3.3
Alphabet Soup

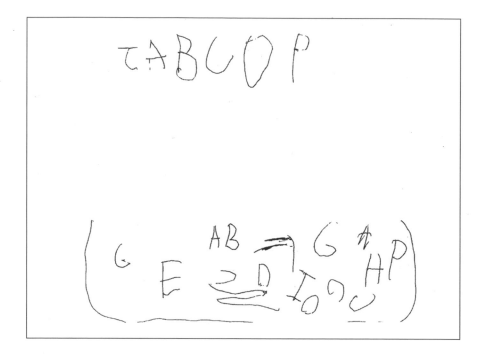

work to a friend or ask for some help recalling a detail, coming up with what happens next, or finding the just-right word. One student will read her work to the publishing volunteer, and I will begin conferencing.

During Quiet Ten, many students draw. I highly recommend this form of prewriting. On the first day of school, if we ask our young students to write, they will give us the symbols they know (or scribbles that look like those symbols). They will write their names, the names of their family members and pets, and any other conventionally spelled words they've practiced. Or, they might simply show off the letters they can write, as Jacob did, telling me that he had written, "alphabet soup" (Figure 3.3).

Too often we want to hothouse them into writing recognizable sentences, so we model what I call "fill in the blank sentences":

I like _____.
I can _____.

This is unnecessary, and it actually backs students up.

Because young children believe that "writing" means wielding a crayon or a pencil, they come to school believing they are writers. For them, drawing and writing are part of the same communication. If you allow your primary students to draw first, they will often provide a complete narrative within the illustration, one with fabulous details. When they move to writing about their picture, the sentences are richer, more sophisticated. And the writing process has true meaning for them.

Based on the work of Martha Horn and Mary Ellen Giacobbe (*Talking, Drawing, Writing: Lessons for Our Youngest Writers*, 2008), Kelsey Frost created three stations in her kindergarten classroom: one where classmates go to talk through their stories, another where students draw their ideas, and the tables where students write. At first Kelsey admits that she feared her students would not move through the stations but would spend most of their time talking (which for kindergarten students could lead them off-task very quickly) or drawing. Much to her surprise, the stations work beautifully. Her kids move from telling stories orally, to drawing, to writing—and when they reach writing they have gained momentum rather than having lost it. Her writing time has extended, and her kids are immensely engaged and proud of their work. Please note: Kelsey does not require that students pass through all three stations sequentially. Some students decide to begin with drawing; others go straight to writing (where they will often draw as well). Kelsey simply gives credence to all of these processes and she spends time in each station asking questions, guiding students to new insights.

One often-reported problem with having students draw first is that some students spend all of their time drawing and too little time composing. This is a different problem for five- to six-year-olds than it is for students who are six and a half to eight. Let's look at the younger set first.

Kindergarten students and some young first graders need help transitioning from illustration to text. Sometimes it's simply a matter of moving from the familiar to the unfamiliar. For others who don't know many letters and their sounds, writing seems like an unwelcome struggle. Even kindergarten students who are well aware of the range of abilities in the classroom fear failure. So how do we help these students?

First of all, I approach with a useful question. I used to say, "Tell me about your picture," but have learned over the years that this request does not always prompt a successful response—especially with students who have processing difficulties. So instead I ask, "What is happening in your picture?" Students respond to this question by telling me a story, and that can give them the confidence to begin recording text.

Many students, however, need more support. For those students, we have a discussion that goes like this:

Me: What's happening in your picture?

Kate: I went outside and it was raining and I saw a rainbow.

Me: Wow! You went outside when it was raining and you saw a rainbow. Would you like to write a word to go with your picture?

Kate: (*Shakes her head.*)

Me: Okay. But if—if you were going to write a word, Kate—just one word—what would it be?

Kate: (*Thinks.*) Rainbow.

Me: Rainbow? You'd write *rainbow*! What a good word.

Kate: (*Nods and smiles at my unexpected enthusiasm.*)

Me: Well, if you were going to write rainbow, where on the page would you put that word?

Kate: (*Slowly points to the top of the page.*)

Me: Right here? You'd put rainbow here!

Kate: (*Nods.*)

Me: Let's do it, Kate. Let's write *rainbow* right here.

At this point I'm going to help Kate stretch the word out. If she can hear the r sound but can't recall the letter that makes that sound, I'll teach it to her. I know that students move from hearing initial consonants, to initial and final, to initial, median, and final. It will be a while before some students will be able to hear vowel sounds. That's okay. We only record the sounds they hear. When students take the time to stretch out a word, they are applying their budding knowledge of phonemes—teaching themselves to read! One ten-minute period of writing demands far more application of phonics than multiple workbook pages.

During my mini-lessons, I often model labeling pictures. I also share picture books by Richard Scarry, which give credence to labeling. I invite students to create labeled pictures just like his. Most students will move quite naturally from labeling their pictures to writing sentences.

Spending most of one's time drawing at the end of first grade or in second grade is usually a different problem. The child who can spend all period working on an illustration is, I'm guessing, right-brain directed. That student knows he or she has a talent for drawing (or a passion at the very least) and is content to spend hours in this activity. So I will often say, feel free to draw during Quiet Ten. When Quiet Ten ends, I would like you to move to writing, but you may return to your drawing tomorrow and every day after that if you wish.

This brings me to a final point about drawing as prewriting. Young students will often draw, then write, return to their drawing to add details, and return to writing to record those details. In other words, when independence is your goal, drawing goes a long way in helping young students remain engaged.

When teaching kindergarten, rather than seating myself at one table, I often move around the room asking students to tell me what is happening in their pictures. As I do so, I help students recognize the letters that make the sounds and encourage them to include the details. What I don't do during this time is spell words for students. (This goes for all grades.) Doing so would transform me from a writing instructor to a human dictionary. When we spell words for them, our students are simply taking dictation. This is not how spelling is learned. Just the opposite. Students best learn to spell by approximating the spelling and then seeing the conventional form.

Even students in primary grades can initially show frustration when I won't spell a word. Chances are they have a very well-meaning parent at home who is more than happy to provide correct spellings. The child has already learned that there is a right and a wrong way and they don't want to be wrong. In this situation, I tell students that when they write the letters that represent the sounds they hear, they are teaching themselves to read, and I don't want to slow that process down for one moment. I tell them that if they have difficulty writing a word that they know is spelled incorrectly, they can, if they wish, circle it or write "sp" above it, and I will assist them with the spelling later. This helps. But what these students really needs is to trust that I mean what I say. So I do lots of mini-lessons in which I model "writing the letters that make the sounds we hear." And it is essential that I refrain from commenting on students' beautifully spelled words and instead praise them for all their spelling attempts. Once they realize that I truly couldn't be more pleased when they've recorded the phonemic spelling of *Tyrannosaurus*, for example, they will feel less locked into using only those words they can manage and will give me the full range of their (usually quite developed) oral vocabulary. Telling parents that I want to see their students' glorious vocabulary also helps some to trust that their children are showing me what they know and that their spelling will develop, over time, into conventional form.

In addition to conducting mini-lessons on labeling pictures and using phonemic spelling, I conduct a lesson on "What to do if you think you're finished with your story," early in the school year. The students and I create a list that will be posted on the wall (but is not needed once writer's workshop has been successfully established). The list usually includes the following:

1. Read your piece to a friend or the class mascot.
2. Read your piece into a "whisper phone" (PVC pipe).
3. Sign up for a conference (and check your work using the editor's checklist).
4. Begin a new piece.
5. Complete a graphic organizer (in the writing center).

Most students end one piece, pull out a new sheet of paper, and start drawing, eager to begin the story they planned on writing next.

Conferencing

As mentioned in the Chapter 1, one of the biggest challenges of supporting your students' self-direction is giving up control. Many teachers, afraid that students will fall through the cracks, assign conference times to their students. And although this appears to be a practice that would reinforce accountability all around, it actually hinders independence. Why? Scheduled conferences take away spontaneity (meeting when a student most needs to meet), any initiation on the student's part, and the motivation to do well every single day. Think about your habits as a learner. If you are taking a course and you meet with your instructor every Thursday—when do you do your best work? Wednesday night, of course. Scheduling weekly conferences in your classroom will roughly have the same effect. On the other hand, when students are given daily access to their writing teacher, they sign up for a conference when it would be most useful and, therefore, most productive.

That's not to say that you will meet with every child every day. (I tried to have five or six solid conferences a day—with a couple of quickie conferences thrown in.) As mentioned in the Chapter 2, I

Regularly scheduled conference times can get in the way of revision. A student comes on Monday. You suggest she add some details. The following Monday she returns. You'd like to look at the details she added and talk about her ending. She pulls out the piece you discussed last time, but a week later this written work has lost all its energy—and she's lost the drive. She is currently engaged in writing a new piece and the opportunity for timely (motivated) revision is gone.

have a sign-up sheet on my board. When one student erases his or her name from the three slots, another may fill his or her name in. Kids often watch the board and know when to step up to the conference table so the conferences flow. Students need not finish a piece to sign up; they may come up during any part of the writing process, though I find primary students to be rather predictable. They get going on a topic, experience excitement, and want to share. They may even think they're done, but are always willing (because the topic feels fresh and exciting) to go back and work on it some more.

What happens if a student never signs up for a conference? Using the record-keeping system I described on page 13, I place his or her name on the board myself. Usually once I've signed a student up, he or she (wanting to have more control over his or her time—it's human nature) will write his or her name on the board the following week.

I will admit that when I first began conducting conferences, I frequently felt overwhelmed. Conferences lasted longer than was productive for the student or for his or her classmates and, paradoxically, I never felt that I'd said enough. What I knew for sure was that I was always behind. Eventually I adopted a procedure (first introduced to me by Paula Flemming, a reading and writing specialist from Peterborough, New Hampshire, who adapted the work from Peter Elbow) that allowed me to stay directed and productive. Later, when I began to organize my instruction around six traits, I added sharper focus to my conferences. For some, the procedure I outline here is going to feel too rigid, too constrictive. And I should point out that I remain natural—saying what I feel most compelled as a fellow writer to say in the moment. But learning to keep conferences focused, explicit, and efficient changed my writing instruction. So perhaps you will look at my procedure and find tips for modifying your own.

Because we view conferences as a limited time to provide one-on-one instruction, we often try to cover way too many skills in a single sitting. We tend to look at the paper in front of us—which reveals all of

Barring injury or fire, students know that they must write a note to interrupt a writing conference.
Some students do take the time to record a question or express a need in a note (which provides additional writing practice), while others find another way of meeting their needs.

its flaws—instead of looking at the very young student. Remember: our job in the writing conference is not to correct a paper, but to teach a budding writer! The aim of the conference should not be to impart all of our knowledge, but to share *one thing* that's going to support genuine writing growth. The procedure is as follows:

1. Set goal
2. Reflect
3. Point
4. Question
5. Teach one skill

Set Goal

I begin a conference by telling the student what we're going to focus on for that day—and in my conferences it's usually a trait. So I might say, "Nathan, we're currently working on ideas, so today I'm going to talk about your focus and quality details." Or I might say, "Yumi, we've been working on voice, so I'm going to point out all of the places where I hear your voice coming through." Setting this goal at the beginning of the conference goes a long way in keeping me on task.

Next, I ask the student to read his or her piece to me. I know that in many cases, it would be far easier and quicker for me to simply read the piece, but I refrain. Not simply to give the student ownership (as my mentor recommended), but to curb my own unfortunate tendencies. Here's the thing. For over twenty years I've known that it's essential when working with *any* writer to respond to what he or she is trying to communicate. In other words, the message should always be honored first. Nevertheless, if I look down at a sheet of writing, my brain becomes a convention detective and notes every missing capital letter, punctuation mark, or misspelling of a frequently used word. Instead of listening to the student's story, I'm focused on the fact that she's still spelling *they* with an *a*, and quite frankly, I'm not hearing a word. I cannot stop this from happening. So instead, I ask students to read their work aloud and that allows me to focus on the content.

Reflect

After the student finishes reading the piece to me, I reflect what I've heard. If Nicholas writes, "My dog sleeps in my bed and takes up all

One of the very best ways to prompt your students to revise is to model the revision of your own work. Do not, however, keep showing them clean drafts. You want to show them pages of works that demonstrate your thinking: crossed-out words and sentences, arrows, carets, notes in the margins. The more regularly you show them your messy drafts, the more apt they will be to revise all on their own.

the room," I say: "Nicholas, you wrote about your dog that sleeps with you and takes up all the room!" This may, at first glance, seem like a totally unnecessary step. But time and time again I'm reminded of how valuable this technique is. First of all, it is amazingly gratifying to hear your words reflected back at you. You'll notice that most of your students grin from ear to ear as you reflect. Second, many students respond to my reflection by extending—orally filling in the gaps. For example, Nicholas might say: "Yeah, and my dog is a Saint Bernard so he comes up to here, and he drools, too." To which I will respond, "Nicholas, those are quality details. How can you add them?"

You, the astute teacher, will notice that I did not say, "Would you like to add them?" which frequently prompts the student to say "No, thanks." But that *how* word—now that's one of the best tools in our kit. Nick will offer his best solution: "I could write that here," or "I could add a spider's leg," (see page 46) to which I will nod and say, "Excellent. Off you go." End of conference.

Remember, Nick only needs to be pointed in the direction of one improvement for now. He will come back when he has proudly made his revision, and we will go on from there. This is the power of reflection.

Point

But what if I had reflected Nick's words and he simply nodded—a sort of "Yup, that's what I wrote." Well then, I just go on to the next step, which is *pointing* to what is working well. Beginning with the positive is not simply a way to buffer the writer for what's coming next (presumably the faults), but a means for helping the writer repeat successes. In fact, I believe that clearly stating what a student has achieved and why is far more useful than identifying all that he or she has yet to learn. The trick is this: we must be very specific. If I simply gush: "Nick, this is wonderful!" he doesn't know why this particular piece is great, he simply knows that he has pleased his teacher. This means that I will probably get a month's worth of stories about his dog. So instead I might say, "You wrote that your dog takes up all the room in your bed. That detail creates a wonderful picture in my mind—a funny picture. I can see you and your dog, and I can't wait to read more." Hopefully Nick will continue to add concrete, vivid details.

Question

After I have pointed, I question the reader. Since Nick didn't offer up additional details in our second scenario, when he responded to the reflection with "Yup," I will solicit some details by asking questions such as: "What type of dog do you have? Is he allowed in your bed? Does he go to bed when you go to bed?" Then I will ask, "How could you add those details?"

During this stage, I help the young writer make revisions, not edits. We are not working on conventions, but on the goal we established at the beginning of the conference; in Nick's case, this was adding details. Being able to articulate what makes good writing (beyond grammar, punctuation, and spelling) is essential for this stage. Many teachers have found that familiarity with the first five of the six traits (ideas, organization, voice, sentence fluency, and word choice) has helped them with knowing how to focus on writing skills.

I often introduce revision techniques to students during the question stage. (Once I have introduced a technique, the student shows it to classmates during the mini-lesson on the following day, so I usually only have to introduce a technique once before it is spreading through the classroom.) I describe some of my favorite approaches in the following sections.

Spider Legs

Purpose: To add information or details.

Directions: Students write a detail on another sheet of paper (the same size and type of paper they have chosen for their draft). They cut out the detail to create a strip (a leg). Then they tape the leg to their original draft—approximately where the detail would be inserted. Students fold the legs over onto the draft page before filing it in the folder. (See Figure 3.4.)

Comments: I love spider legs because rather than simply adding details at the end of what they've already written, writers think about the very best placement for the detail.

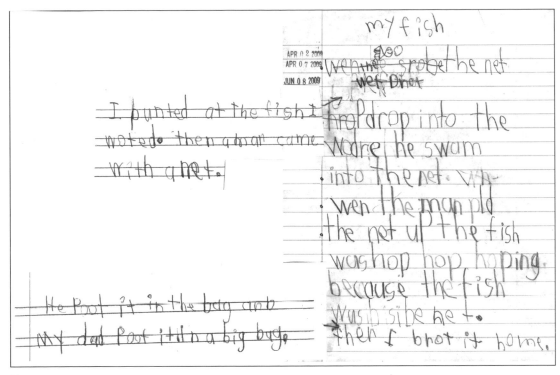

Figure 3.4
Spider Legs Aid
Revision

Asterisks

Purpose: To add information or details.

Directions: Students locate the precise point where they wish to add information to their draft and write a numbered asterisk (*1 at the first place they want to add information, *2 at the next place, and so on). They then take a separate sheet of paper, write the corresponding numbered asterisks, and write the text to be added. When reading aloud, students go back and forth from their original draft to the page of additions.

Comments: Do not, at some point, ask young students to "write a clean draft" incorporating their additions. This back and forth is too difficult and will halt the use of this fabulously useful teaching technique. If the piece is published, a volunteer types the revisions into the final document.

Surgery

Purpose: To reorder information or provide room for important details.

Directions: Students cut up their draft in order to change the sequence of the information. Once they have reordered the information, they glue or tape it in the new order on another sheet of paper.

Comments: Often students create one long list without any quality details: "Mandy wanted to buy a dog. First she tried a lemonade stand but that didn't work. Next she tried doing chores, but that that didn't work either." In these cases, I tell the student that she has the bones of her story and now needs to add the details. I help her cut the bones up, paste one bone at the top of each sheet of paper, and encourage her to elaborate with details that will provide the reader with a clear picture of what is happening.

Teach One Skill

Before the writer leaves the conference, I focus on one (yes, just one) new skill—most often a convention. The skill taught is recorded on the student's checklist (see Figure 2.6) with the assumption that he or she will check work and apply the convention before coming to the next conference.

Why not more than one skill? Because the young student will not retain the teaching, and I am not only wasting his or her time but also depriving the rest of my class of writing instruction time. When observing others' conferences, I often detect a moment when the teacher has gone too far. It's the instant when the pencil has magically moved from the child's hand to the teacher's, and he or she, sensing time is running out, is making marks all over the paper. The student is watching, but the light has gone out.

So when do I focus on necessary conventions? Before a student takes work to publishing, we'll have an editing conference where we focus only on punctuation, grammar, and spelling. In this instance we will work for as long as the student is engaged and learning. Publishing is a time to celebrate success, so I'm careful not to cross that very fragile line from celebration to discouragement. Focusing on too many conventions at once, even during an editing conference, can give the student the counterproductive message that writing has a gazillion rules to remember: "So why bother?" One trick that was passed along to me by teachers at the Durham Elementary School in Durham, Maine, was to place a dot in the margin before every line that has an error in conventions. I love this idea. When we wield our red pens on our students work and show them where they need to make a change, they make the corrections without thinking hard about what we've taught them. With the dot system, they have to recall what they know. They also strive to have fewer dots placed on their work next time.

Author's Chair

Each day three children, and only three children, share their work with the whole class. I limit it to three because after three readers, no one gets an audience; other students check out. In fact, if a fourth child gets up to read, chances are even you are not listening. Instead you are using stares and hand gestures to coerce distracted students into paying attention. My second rule: Students may sign up only once a week, which means each child gets to share every week and a half or so.

I use a process during author's chair similar to the one I use during writing conferences, thus reinforcing the language and procedures.

The child, seated in the special author's chair, reads her work, and everyone applauds. Then she asks, "Any pointing?" and classmates comment positively. Initially, of course, many of the "points" sound like this: "I like that you wrote about your dog. I have a dog . . ." But I also raise my hand, and in the primary classroom, I am always called on. I then model pointing by reinforcing the qualities that make good writing. So I might mention something like the following:

- "You chose to write about the first time you ate pudding. What a fine, manageable topic!" (We spend a lot of time talking about topics that are too big.)
- "You wrote: 'When I went underwater, my eyes stung.' That is a lovely detail that allows me to imagine your story."
- "You began your story with a sound. Oooh, did that hook me! I wanted to hear more."
- "When you said, 'God and Jessie made a good team,' I smiled because that sounds just like you, Ian. That's your unique voice coming through."
- "Your sentence, 'My kite flip flapped like a bird,' sounds like a poem. Very fluent!"

Eventually the kids will begin to emulate me when responding to their classmates, especially when I give little nods or sounds of approval as they do so. They become the ones reinforcing the strategies —reinforcing what constitutes good writing each and every day.

Next the author asks, "Any questions?" I know many teachers encourage classmates to offer suggestions, and I think this can also be very productive. But I prefer questions because they allow writers to maintain a greater sense of ownership. Instead of a classmate saying, "You should begin in a more exciting way," he or she says, "Why did you decide to begin your story that way?" This gives the author a chance to think about his or her writing choices and, in the process, discover ways to improve them.

Granted, young writers don't always answer the questions in the most scholarly way. We often hear, "It's what I thought of," and some of our students in the audience get stuck asking the very same question day after day. However, don't despair. The value of questioning is actually more evident during writing time. Picture the young writer beginning a new piece. She starts to write the typical, "One day," and suddenly the voice of her classmate, Joely, comes into her head. Joely *always* asks "Why did you decide to begin your story that way?" So our young writer crosses out "One day" and writes, "Where are you going with that fish?" She's going to call on Joely during author's chair, and she'll have her answer at the ready.

I also model effective questioning during author's chair. In addition, I have sticky notes in hand, and when a student asks a particularly astute question, perhaps a clarifying question or a question about process, I write it down on a sticky note and hand it to the author. This accomplishes two goals. It tells the writer that she or he just heard a question worth paying attention to, and it reinforces the student who asked the perceptive question. Don't write down every question that is asked—only those that have a very specific and positive influence on the piece. As you remember from Mr. Skinner, intermittent reinforcement is the most powerful (1964).

So, you ask, what does author's chair have to do with student independence? Everything. Writers are motivated by audience. A single teacher's response does not make an audience. Students will write for longer periods, use livelier language, include dazzling details, and search for their unique voice when performing for classmates. That's what an author reading is after all: a performance.

Chapter 4

Mini-Lessons That Build Independence

My final student-teaching practicum was in a third-grade classroom. For an entire semester I observed and taught eight-year-olds. I became increasingly familiar with their development and needs, and with the third-grade curriculum. I was thrilled then when I was offered a position teaching third grade in a nearby town. When the joy of being hired calmed down, I called my supervising teacher. In addition to offering her congratulations, she assured me I that I couldn't be more suited for the job.

"But, but . . ." I stammered.

"But, what?" she asked.

"But what do I do on the first day?"

You may feel a bit like I did jumping into writer's workshop. You now know the tone of the workshop and what it looks like when it's up and running—when it's well established—but how do you start?

Initially, many of your mini-lessons will focus on creating a community of writers and the management of your writer's workshop. You might consider brief lessons, for example, on the use of the writing center and folders and on the conferencing procedure. In addition, you will want to do a good deal of modeling of drawing as prewriting, topic selection, the use of phonemic spelling, labeling pictures (especially in kindergarten and first grade), and what to do if you've completed a piece.

The following is a sample of the mini-lessons I might do during the first month of school. You may pick and choose and you need not adhere to this order. Also, it's important to say that your student's writing development—*their* needs—should drive your planning, not this book or any other. Your students will show you what they're on the verge of learning, and when you follow their lead, your mini-lessons can't fail.

Week 1
- Model drawing a picture story; label one item by stretching out a word and recording the letters that represent sounds heard.
- Introduce folders and the date stamp.
- Take a tour of the writing center.
- Read an everyday experience story. Invite students to share connections. Record them in a list.
- Choose a short writing sample to project for the whole class to see. Ask, "What did we learn about this writer?" Point out that we learn about the lives and ideas of others through their writing. (Samples should not be from your class. For a list of places to find writing samples, see the sidebar on page 68).

Week 2
- Read *Wilfrid Gordon McDonald Partridge* by Mem Fox (1985). Share a basket of objects. Tell your stories. (See mini-lesson "Writing from Memories" on page 58.)
- Model writing a sentence (or sentences, depending on your class) beneath a picture.
- Remind students that they are experts on many things. Perhaps they have a collection of some sort (second graders are natural collectors), have spent lots of time participating in a favorite activity, or have learned a good deal about something—say, dinosaurs, recycling, or saving pennies. Begin a list titled "Things We Know About" and post it in the classroom. You might begin with your own (highly relatable) areas of expertise: family chores, getting kids to eat their vegetables, riding the subway, things that worry you.

- Model writing a note (to be used when you're in a conference) (see sidebar on page 43).
- Create a list titled "What to Do If You Finish a Piece" and post it on the wall.

Week 3

- Read *A House for Hermit Crab* by Eric Carle (1991). Students add details to an outline of a house (see mini-lesson "Adding Details" on page 63).
- Interactive writing: retell a class activity. Add specific, quality details. Model revision techniques such as the caret, arrows, and crossing off as you go.
- Share a piece of your writing that is unclear. Encourage students to ask questions. Later, rewrite the piece with questions answered.
- Share your revised piece, modeling the importance of thinking about audience.
- Modeled writing: demonstrate moving from list to focused topic (see mini-lesson "Using 'Binoculars' to Focus a Topic" on page 61).

Week 4

- Read *No, David!* by David Shannon (1998) and ask the students, "What did this author choose to focus on?" (*David's misbehavior, following rules.*) Eventually you will be able to ask students, "What did you choose to focus on in your writing?"
- Project a writing sample on the board. Ask, "Did this author focus on one topic? If so, what topic did the author focus on?"
- Model the use of a web graphic organizer for focus (see mini-lesson "Focus Web" on page 66).
- Introduce the concept of using "binoculars" for quality details (see "Extension" on page 62).
- Provide students with a topic grid. Basically, it's a box-grid with six to nine suggested topic areas. For example, your grid could include family, friends, school, animals, worst mistake, biggest success, ouch! and so on. Students check or color a box when they've written a piece that fits that category. (Model the use of your own grid. After writing a piece about your father, for example, put a check in the "family" box. Remind students to focus on a small idea within the large topic.)

Using an Organizing Structure for Your Mini-Lessons

Notice that during week 3, I begin to teach students about *ideas* (the first trait, according to six traits writing), which can be subdivided into three important concepts: (1) writing with clarity, (2) focusing on a manageable topic, and (3) writing with quality details. (Quality details are those that go beyond the obvious or general. "We had fun," is a generic detail. "We played Red Rover and I broke through my friends' arms," is a quality detail.) I recommend choosing an organizing principle for your lessons—be it six traits, genre (personal narrative, how-to, poetry), or units of study.

When I first began teaching, my organizing principle was thematic units. Oh, those were the days! We would move from a study of bears to outer space to dinosaurs, integrating literacy, math, and science. It was fun, it was imaginative, and it provided students lots of hooks for learning. However, I was still using what I call the buffet method of teaching writing: details on Monday, great leads on Tuesday, lively verbs on Wednesday, proper nouns on Thursday, focus on Friday. In other words, writing skills were presented in a willy-nilly fashion (all skills demonstrated in my bear books, but willy-nilly just the same). When using the buffet method, students do not have enough time to practice skills—to build upon the knowledge and make it theirs—and teachers tend to both teach and assess those skills that they, as teachers, understand best.

Of course, writing traits are interconnected. It's hard to focus on voice without talking about quality details, word choice, and fluency. However, by clustering lessons, we ensure that our students (and we) develop all of our writing muscles evenly. Right now, you may be the King or Queen of Organization. Your students leave your classroom knowing how to write with a solid beginning, middle, and end. However, they may not be able to identify fluency. An organizing structure helps provide you and students with a road map that takes in *all* the sights in depth, not just breadth.

Teaching Conventions

You may wonder why I'm not focusing more on conventions in the first few weeks. Where are the lessons on writing from left to right, spaces between words, and capital letters? As you'll recall, I do focus on conventions at the start of each morning meeting when examining the message. Also, I conduct more convention mini-lessons as the year gets going, always reminding students that we write for an audience and therefore want to make our communications understood. However, too much emphasis on conventions will prevent your students from becoming fully engaged, independent writers.

Think of your finest hour in writing, that one moment perhaps when a teacher read your work to the class, your mother called your aunt to read your piece aloud, the local newspaper ran your letter, or you won your high school essay contest. Were you most proud of your comma placement? Your ability to use the semicolon successfully? Of course not. You were pleased that others felt you had something important, interesting, or funny to say. Your students will become engaged in their work when they are taken seriously as writers, when they feel as if what they recorded on paper made someone else smile from ear to ear.

And since we're on the subject of too great a focus on conventions, let me share another view. Learning to write conventionally, like learning to speak properly, has a developmental sequence. We know that primary students, that is, those who have moved beyond scribbles to writing letters and words, *usually* begin by using all capital letters, which are easier for children whose fine motor skills are just developing. They often write strings of letters with mostly consonants because it's the consonant sounds they hear. As they become aware of spacing, they may put dots or lines between their words. When students begin to use more lowercase letters, there will be reversals, especially of the letters *b* and *d*. All of this is expected—and temporary. You could provide mini-lessons that show students how to use two fingers to space their words or teach them the trick of imagining a bed to recall which way the first and last letters face, but why use your valuable teaching time on something that will (unless there is a learning disability) correct itself? I've actually seen kindergarten students write in columns—a result of placing two fingers between each word, before the child was ready for this practice.

Teaching these conventions is akin, I believe, to a mother correcting her child each time he says, "Dada." Imagine a mother saying, "No, sweetie. It's 'Daddy.' Say '*Daddy.*'" Mothers don't do this because they honor and delight in all of the stages of speech development. They trust that "Dada" will become "Daddy" all too quickly. I love seeing those little dots between words in my students' writing and know that those dots, too, will soon disappear.

That's why our mini-lessons must always convey the attitude "We are *all* writers"—not when you master sentence structure or capital letters, but now. Every day. You show your young students what professional writers do because you truly believe they are up to the task of emulating these authors.

Teaching Strategies for Mini-Lessons

Many teachers new to writer's workshop become overwhelmed with the idea of providing writing mini-lessons five days a week. I'm often asked, "Where do I find all those lessons on voice?" No matter which form of scaffolding you choose, it may help to conducting mini-lessons that incorporate these five teaching strategies:

1. Mentor texts: Examine published writing to learn craft.
2. Modeled writing: Share your writing (often writing in front of the students) and welcome their feedback.
3. Interactive writing: You and students compose together.
4. Graphic organizers: Collect observations, strategies, and thoughts about writing and organize them visually.
5. Examining writing (not your students'): Project writing samples on a screen and discuss the presence or lack of a trait.

Sometimes a mini-lesson incorporates more than one of these strategies, as I demonstrate in using Eric Carle's (1991) *A House for Hermit Crab* to move into an interactive writing lesson (page 63) or *McDuff Moves In* by Rosemary Wells (2005) to complete a graphic organizer (page 59). Further explanation of each strategy follows.

Mentor Texts

Learning writing skills within the context of fabulous (and fabulously written) literature helps build a genuine awe of craft as well as a sense of belonging to a fun, interesting, imaginative community. "Mo Willems is an author," thinks the admiring second grader, "and so am I."

Other kids were raising their hands. Dolores Starbuckle jumped up and down on her knees and waved her arms like a willow tree in a windstorm. Ms. Janice motioned for Dolores to sit back down.

Figure 4.1
Andy Shane and the Very Bossy Dolores Starbuckle

Many teachers attend conferences and search the Internet for lists of mentor texts and ways to use them to model fine writing. I have nothing against these lists (in fact I've written many), but they can cause frustration. Often a teacher discovers that her school library carries only one or two of the titles on the list, or a librarian painstakingly categorizes literature in her collection according to six traits only to discover that the teachers have difficulty knowing *how* the person who initially tagged the book as a good model for word choice would use the book with primary students. So study the lists if it helps, but in addition, learn how to examine the literature in your classroom and in the books you love to identify author's craft. It's not as hard as you might think.

Figure 4.1 is an interior page from one of my books, *Andy Shane and the Very Bossy Dolores Starbuckle* (2005). Look at the text on this page and imagine (beyond conventions) what you might focus on in a mini-lesson.

Using the page shown in Figure 4.1, you might focus on the following:

- Word choice and how vivid verbs bring energy to writing: *raising, jumped, waved, motioned.*
- How quality details ("Dolores jumped up and down on her knees and waved her arms like a willow tree in a windstorm") help the reader picture the story. (I always tell young students that it's the job of the writer to create a movie in the mind of a reader.)
- The way in which authors *show* what a character is feeling rather than *telling* us. We know that Dolores is excited and that Ms. Janice wishes she would be a little less so, simply by their actions.

Once you've chosen your writing organizational structure (whether it be genre, six traits, or some other structure), prepare file folders. For example, I use six traits, so I have one folder marked "Ideas," another "Organization," and so on. As you read books to your students, you will no doubt think, "Oh, this is a great example of . . ." Write the down the title and toss the slip of paper into the corresponding folder. The following year, you will have lots of familiar mentor texts at your fingertips as you plan your mini-lessons.

Three lessons from a single paragraph! Give it a try and you'll see that you'll be able to do this with any book in your classroom. You'll want to preview books ahead of time. My passage would be a fine selection for verb choice, but not for adjectives. Make sure the book you select is a good model of the skill you'll be teaching that day. The better you become at identifying author's craft in the stories and nonfiction you love, the more confident you will be during your mini-lessons. The students will pick up on your love and admiration for a book and will share their appreciation as well.

In fact, you might want to end your mini-lesson with an invitation to students: "As you're reading today, see if you can't find examples of vivid verbs, quality details, or show, don't tell." The students will come running with text that can be used in subsequent mini-lessons. And how proud the student will be when you use the book that *he or she* found!

When choosing literary mentors, don't forget to include nonfiction. Many young students gravitate toward factual reading and writing and will incorporate both the tone and elements of nonfiction into their writing. When teaching expository writing—how-to's, reports, persuasive letters, and essays—it's essential that students have had lots of exposure to these genres.

Sample Mentor Text Lessons

Writing from Memories

On Hand: The book *Wilfrid Gordon McDonald Partridge* by Mem Fox (1985) and a basket of objects that not only spark my childhood stories, but hopefully my students' memories as well. At one time or another I have had in my basket: a scrap of silk, a flashlight, a worn teddy bear, a child's ring, and a cat's collar.

Mini-Lesson: I read *Wilfrid Gordon McDonald Partridge*, a story about a little boy who brings a basket of objects to Miss Nancy, an old woman who has lost her memory. Miss Nancy takes the objects out of the basket one by one and consequently remembers stories from her childhood.

Then I bring *my* basket out. I, too, lift objects into the air and tell my own stories. For example, I show the scrap of silk and tell students how my parents had a silky blanket on their bed that my brothers and I fought over. One day when we were tussling—each pulling in a different direction, the coveted blanket tore.

Or I tell them about the time when my then husband and I took our kids on a camping trip. My two-year-old son woke in his portable crib at five a.m. Desperate to get more sleep, I passed him our heavy camping flashlight to play with. He lifted that flashlight, leaned over the railing of his crib, and dropped it on my husband's head!

You probably know what my primary students are doing while I'm telling my stories: They're waving their hands in the air, desperate to share the memory that my story helped them to recall. Instead of encouraging them to tell their stories (though you could invite a couple if you wish), I have them identify the topic of their story and send them off to write. They practically run to the writing center for their folders.

I have never found that the students don't relate to my objects or stories. The slip of silk solicits wonderfully detailed narratives about beloved "blankies" and often the heart-pulling story of having to part with that security object. One student will say, "I'm going to write about the blanket I had as a baby," and suddenly four more hands shoot up. Those kids are going to write about their "binkies," their "nappies," and their "night-nights.") The flashlight story reminds students of all the "funny things I did as a baby" stories that their parents and relatives have told them over and over again.

Extension: Many teachers extend this lesson by inviting students to bring in an object that prompts a story they can tell and later write about.

Sensory Words

On Hand: The book *McDuff Moves In* by Rosemary Wells (2005) and a whiteboard.

Mini-Lesson: Remind students that when we write with quality details, the reader feels as if he or she is right there, experiencing the story firsthand. One way that authors make the story come alive for us is through the use of sensory details. Draw a four-column chart on the board. At the top of the columns write: *hear, feel, smell*, and *taste*. (Notice that I did not include the sense of sight. Most writing is so visual that you would be stopping to record every other word of a story.)

Tell students that you are going to reread *McDuff Moves In* and on this reading, you would like the students to stop you every time they hear a word that allows them to use one of the senses listed on the chart. Record the words in the proper column. Some words, such as *sausages*, will appear in more than one column (smell, taste). Point out that although most objects can be touched, the feelings words tell how something feels: *soft, fuzzy, scratchy, warm, wet*.

Invite students to include sensory words in their writing that day.

Extension: The next day, provide students with a blank organizer like the one you drew on the board. Ask them to look back on the writing they did the day before and record any sensory words they used in their writing. Those that have few (or no sensory words) will be inclined to revise their writing to include more.

Modeled Writing

It's Monday morning and I'm madly scrambling through my professional books for an introductory lesson on quality details. Certainly someone has the quintessential lesson for introducing the concept. It seems I have to cast a wide net to find the "just-right" lesson. However, I remember that modeling a trait (and our thinking around that trait) is truly one of the most effective ways of teaching writing skills, so I give up trying to find a lesson someone else has written and sit myself in front my students to show them how I write with details instead.

I need to show students that the right details can transform a piece. In front of them, I write something banal:

It's peaceful on my back porch. I love to sit there.

I then say, "Oh, I can see that I haven't created a picture in the reader's mind at all. I want to write a piece that makes the reader feel as if he or she is sitting on the porch with me." I flip the chart paper and write the following, explaining my thinking as I write:

There are three chairs on my back porch. One of them, a little white rocker, is my favorite. I pitch back and forth listening to the sound of the . . . ["What is the curved part of a rocking chair leg called? *Runners, I think.*"] . . . runners on the wooden floor. Above me, a maple tree spreads its leafy arms, creating a canopy. A chickadee flits from limb to limb.

"Is this better?" I ask the students.
"Yes," they say. "We can see your back porch now."
Don't hesitate to use your own writing to teach craft.

Sample Modeled Writing Lesson

Using "Binoculars" to Focus a Topic

On Hand: A pair of binoculars and an easel pad.

Mini-Lesson: "Put on your binoculars" becomes a metaphor for both focus and the inclusion of quality details in my classes, but I don't want to assume that my primary students have had experience with binoculars and that they truly know what binoculars can do. So I bring a pair in and give each student a turn looking through them before beginning my morning meeting.

During morning meeting, I tell students that I'm going to begin by writing a list. Many primary students, through training or by nature, make lists. I want to help them to differentiate between a list and a focused topic. So I write my "I like" list:

I like my family.
I like my friends.
I like my house.
I like my dogs.
I like to write.

However, I say, during writing time I don't want to write a list. I want to write with focus. So, I'm going to take out my handy binoculars (here I don't bring out the real binoculars, but use my hands to create pretend ones, causing all of the students to create their own pretend binoculars—perfect!) and tell them that I'm going to choose one of the items on my list to focus on. I circle one of the items, such as "I like my dogs," turn the page on the easel pad, and write several focused sentences about my dogs, complete with quality details. "There," I say. "Now I've written a focused piece."

Ask students to use their binoculars again to tell you what they will focus on during writing time today.

Extension: Use the pretend binoculars to focus on quality details as well. (This concept is inspired by lessons in the highly recommended *Reviser's Toolbox* by Barry Lane [1999].) Put on your pretend binoculars and say to students: "I see a field." Then "focus" your binoculars and look again. "There is a cow in the field." Focus again: "The cow is black and white and chewing her cud." Focus: "There is a fly on the cow's nose and it's washing its feet." Help students to understand that zooming in leads to quality details.

Choose a different setting—a road, a room, the beach—and invite students to take turns using their binoculars to report on details.

You'll find that students, when examining writing that lacks details, will often say, "The writer needs to put on her binoculars."

Interactive Writing

Do you remember playing the game in which each person begins a story and then passes the paper on until everyone else has had the opportunity to add a sentence? Kids love this game because of the funny twists and turns each story takes; they also love collaborating. And why not? Collaborating brings fresh ideas and the joy of creating something together.

This is true of interactive writing as well. With this strategy, students compose together. As the teacher you inquire, guide, and shape. Purists of this technique would say that the students are the scribes—the marker is in their hands. However, there are times when I know the lesson will move at the right pace if I'm the one doing the recording. (In the primary grades, I will often have students record a word or two, but seldom an entire sentence, as others will lose interest.)

The beauty of the interactive writing is that not only do your students teach one another (why is it that lessons are learned more quickly when modeled by classmates?), but all students experience a sense of pride in the resulting product. This is essential for those students who, for whatever reason, have to work harder at writing.

Sample Interactive Writing Lesson

Adding Details

On Hand: *A House for Hermit Crab* by Eric Carle (1991), a whiteboard, and an easel pad.

Mini-Lesson: Read the book (preferably the day before, which will allow more time for writing during this lesson). Remind students that Hermit Crab thought his house looked plain, so he added lots of sea creatures to give it color and interest. When we write, we add lots of details to give our work interest.

Next, draw a large square on the whiteboard to represent a house. Point out that presently, this is a very plain house. Invite students to come up one by one and add a detail. Hand off the marker until each child has had a turn. Initially you'll get predictable details: roof, windows, door. But after these are done students will begin to add more imaginative details.

When every child has had a turn, go to your easel pad and, together, write a paragraph about the newly decorated house that includes every single detail.

Extension: In winter, draw three circles to represent a snowperson. Repeat the lesson, allowing students to add details.

Graphic Organizers

If you are like me, you never stop admiring the amazing details included in Nicola Davies's nonfiction or the voice in Kate McMullen's picture books, and you share these observations with your students often. Nevertheless, I fear there are times when, especially for our strong visual learners, we sound a little like the adults in a Charlie Brown TV special: WAWAWA stunning WAWAWA listen to this WAWAWA . . .

And that's why I love graphic organizers: less talk and more visual representation. They allow students to make their own connections as we pull together data, data that guides them to new understandings. Graphic organizers provide schemata: a way of structuring information or arranging key concepts into a pattern, enhancing understanding and application.

Students who might not otherwise participate in a discussion will offer information for a graphic organizer. Unlike worksheets, graphic organizers are open-ended and therefore, I validate all responses. If a student gives me a response for which there is no box (or column, circle, path, etc.), I create one. If I were collecting lively verbs, for example, and a child provided a word that was not an action word, I might create a new space titled "Words that remind us of verbs."

Why not just reject the sometimes seemingly incorrect response? Because in writing, participation and risk taking are more important than being right. And often, if I take the time to question the student's response, he or she shares a legitimate line of thinking that was not immediately apparent. If young students are hesitant to participate (usually the first time they've done a graphic organizer with me), I put students' initials next to their responses. Now all hands go up!

As mentioned in Chapter 2, I always model the use of a graphic organizer with the whole group before handing it to individuals or placing them in the writing center. For this initial presentation, they can be duplicated on overhead transparencies or quickly sketched on your easel pad or whiteboard. What's amazing is that if you use organizers on a regular basis, students—even primary students—will begin to invent their own.

Sample Lessons Using Graphic Organizers

Idea Map

On Hand: Whiteboard.

Mini-Lesson: At times your class will be buzzing with the energy of winning topics, and then there will be lulls when it seems as if all the familiar subjects

Figure 4.2
An Idea Map

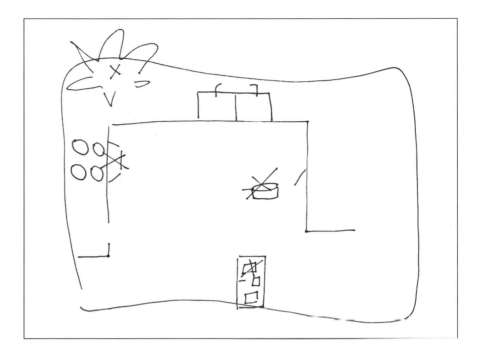

have been beaten to death. In these instances (or when you're getting your writer's workshop up and running) modeling an idea map always reignites students, prompting fresh and lively narratives.

Tell students that you came to school not knowing what you were going to write today. So, you've decided to create an idea map. Draw the outline of a map on the whiteboard (Figure 4.2).

Now tell them that in order to create an idea map, you need to select a place you know well: your kitchen, the playground, your back-yard, your daycare, or your grandmother's home—any of these will work as long as it's a place where you've spent lots of time.

Choose a setting and begin to sketch the physical landmarks on the map. Place an X each and every time your drawing prompts the recollection of a story. For example, if I were drawing a map of my kitchen, I would say: "The cupboards go here. Oh! When my children were small, and I needed to accomplish something, I would open the cupboard doors and let them pull out all the pots and pans—X marks the spot. I have a story

I've written the following books that provide graphic organizers for writing mini-lessons:

Trait-Based Writing Graphic Organizers and Mini-Lessons: 20 Graphic Organizers with Mini-Lessons to Help Students Brainstorm, Organize Ideas, Draft, Revise, and Edit (2008).
Graphic Organizers for the Overhead: Reading and Writing (2007).
The Big Book of Reproducible Graphic Organizers, with Dottie Raymer (1999).

here." I keep filling in the map this way, recalling the day I was pureeing soup for guests and the cover came off the food processor, covering the walls with soup, or the time the taco shells caught fire in the oven and we had to call the fire department. Even my daughter's drawing on the front of the refrigerator suggests a story.

When you have marked your map with four or five *X*s, invite students to draw an idea map of their own.

Extension: Provide students with an outline of a child's body. (I search for a gingerbread person outline on the Web and download the image.) Encourage students to draw a Band-Aid everywhere on the body where they've experienced a boo-boo. You will get many great "owie" stories with lots of interesting details.

Focus Web

On Hand: Whiteboard and marker.

Mini-Lesson: Draw a circle in the center of the board. Choose a topic that is too unwieldy, for example: "weather." Next, ask students to brainstorm everything they could tell a reader about weather. Students might begin recalling types of weather (*rain, snow, sleet, hail, hurricanes, tornadoes*), move on to clothing (*raincoat, umbrella, boots, mittens*), and then think of the less obvious (*weather forecasts, radar, tornado sirens*, etc.). Keep adding content until the students seem to truly exhaust all ideas.

Then say, "Wow, weather is too big a topic. If we were to write about this topic, I fear we wouldn't have any quality details at all." (Anything less than a book would be one long list). Model choosing one of the subtopics in your web, perhaps *rain*. In my class we talk about choosing the Goldilocks idea: one that's not too big, nor too small, but just right. With students, write an interactive paragraph on this topic that includes specific, sensory details.

Extension: Suggest students make a web for one of the following "too-large" topics and then choose a smaller idea to develop in their writing:

- My family
- My vacation
- Things I can do

Examining Writing

One of the most effective ways to teach writing (and one that is seldom used) is projecting sample writing on a screen and encouraging students to discuss one specific aspect of craft. Before I go any further, let me stress that you don't want to use your own students' writing. You don't want your students' anxiety raised each and every time you mention their names for fear that it's going to be a moment of shame instead of fame. (Do feel free, however, to show your students writing as a positive model on a consistent basis—just don't offer it up for discussion.)

Project the writing and tell students which written quality you want them to examine. You do not want to begin by saying, "So. What do you think of this writing?" If you do, students will offer up many responses on disparate areas—often focusing on the conventions, length, or penmanship. This might feel gratifying until you realize that all of these different comments dilute the mini-lesson and have very little effect on the application of skills. Instead, ask one question, such as:

- Is this writing clear?
- Did the author include quality details?
- Did the author of this piece focus on one topic?
- Does the lead hook you?
- Is the piece well organized?
- Does the ending work?
- Does this piece have voice?
- Does the writing flow?

I often have primary students answer my question first with a thumbs-up, thumbs-down, or the ever popular waving thumbs for sort of. Then we discuss the trait, or lack thereof, beginning with those students who have their thumbs up. (If you begin with students who feel the trait is lacking, those with their thumbs up will no longer want to respond.) The discussion proceeds in this way:

Me: Did the author focus on one topic? (*Wait for thumbs.*) Sujata, you say yes. Tell us more.
Sujata: Well, it's sort of like an all-about-me book.
Me: So you feel the author is writing about himself—that he has chosen *himself* as the topic.

Sujata: (*Nods.*)

Me: Who else had his or her thumb up?

Jason: He's sort of writing about things he likes, except when he tells us about the movie that was boring.

Me: So you feel, Jason, his topic is *things he likes.*

(*This response prompts all the kids who had thumbs down and are dying to have their say to wave their arms in the air. I call on Mandy.*)

Mandy: I don't think he focuses at all. First he's talking about school, then foods he likes, and then he starts talking about that boring movie.

Me: So, you don't think his piece is focused. What do you think the author could do to improve this piece?

Mandy: He could pick one of those things and write about it with details.

Marcus: He needs to use the binoculars.

Me: That's a good thing for us to keep in mind as we write today . . .

Notice that I never say which group of students is "right." As with graphic organizers, you want to validate every response, allowing them to grow into a genuine discussion. The more you listen (and refrain from instructing), the more participation you'll get. And the more students participate, the more they will understand the trait and apply it to their own writing. Remember, students learn more when they become accustomed to listening to each other.

When choosing samples, exhibit a range of writing ability. Those that would receive a low rubric score allow your students to feel smug as they offer up good writing advice. Those that would receive a high rubric score become a road map—a vision of how to accomplish fine writing.

I have only a few memories of learning to write in elementary school, but I do remember one day in third grade. We were given the prompt "A grandmother is . . ." I can't recall a single word of my own draft, but at the end of our writing time, our teacher read us an article written by a nine-year-old in 1955. The piece had voice, humor, and perfectly selected details.

 So where do you find writing samples?

* Ask your colleagues for writing samples (take the names off). You don't need to use samples from your own grade. I often use pieces written by third or fourth graders in primary classrooms.
* Search for *anchor papers* for standardized assessments on the Web. You'll find that many school districts are posting writing samples for the use of assessment practice.
* Save copies of your students' work this year to use next year.
* Use samples from the book *Writing Lessons for the Overhead: Grades 2–3* by Lola M. Schaefer (2006).

Forty years later, I can still remember one line: "Usually grandmas are fat, but not too fat to tie kids' shoes." (Perhaps because this line described my beloved grandma.) I was in awe of what was possible.

* * *

As mentioned in the beginning of the chapter, allow your students' written work to guide the planning of your mini-lessons. Also, reinforce positive application of writing skills and revision techniques by asking students to coteach mini-lessons with you. Students are more apt to try new strategies when they have been modeled by classmates. Before long, you'll have more mini-lessons than days in the month, but that's a fine problem to have.

Chapter 5

A Year of Mini-Lessons for Growing Writers

When thinking about a year of writing lessons, we need to give equal weight to craft, conventions, genre, and writing process. There is often a temptation, when teaching very young children, to overemphasize one of these areas and not give enough attention to the others. Many primary teachers (especially with the onslaught of early childhood testing) feel it's their responsibility to get all of their kids producing clean products, that is, sentences with capital letters, punctuation, and attention to conventional spelling. Certainly we can hothouse our youngest writers, getting them to produce something that looks good on the page, but these modeled sentences, which often entail copying, have very little to do with real writing. So, yes, we need to teach conventions—but not make them the standards by which we measure all writing progress.

At the other end of the spectrum are teachers who celebrate young students' ideas but are loathe to ask primary students to revise. Again, I feel the need to emphasize that revision is *not* correcting "mistakes" by copying work over to a clean draft—I, too, disagree with this practice. These teachers often have come to view suggestions for revision—adding details, changing order, crossing off unneeded information—as negative criticism But successful writing requires the understanding that writing is all about making choices. We try something, it may or may not work, but we know that we can make changes; our writing can always be improved. This is the foundation for risk taking essential for writing growth. Young children should play with their writing in the same way they might play with sand or clay. Revision should always be honored, applauded, celebrated: He is a writer for he is the one who revises.

Unfortunately, I can't map out a clear scope and sequence for teaching conventions and revision. The timing of these lessons should always be differentiated, dependent upon the unique developmental needs of your students. I suggest giving daily attention to print through your morning message, with occasional mini-lessons that focus on conventions and revision as your students show readiness for them. And remember, every time you model writing you are modeling conventions along with the trait discussed. What I can give you is a suggested sequence for the teaching of craft and genre, but even these suggestions should be treated as a loose outline. If in October, for example, you have students who have begun to write "choose your own adventure stories" and classmates want to join in, I certainly would follow their lead with mini-lessons on crafting story. After all, nothing supports writing growth more than passion.

One thing is for certain, whether you teach kindergarten or second grade: Your primary students are very different writers in September than they are in January. First-grade teachers have always talked of the big leap that seems to occur right after winter break. Emerging writers have moved from letterlike symbols to connecting letters to sounds. Transitional writers, through a combination of phonemic and conventional spelling, are expressing multiple ideas in sentences. Fluent writers are making increasingly sophisticated choices in craft. Because our students' skill sets are so different in the beginning of the year compared to the end, I suggest spiraling writing content—that is, introducing an important skill such as incorporating quality details in September, and then spending significant time revisiting the same skill four months later.

So, this chapter is a map of sorts. A GPS, perhaps. One you follow while always listening for the ever-present voice that tells you, "recalculating." Use the mini-lesson ideas that follow, but remember that it's *always* your students' work that should dictate the direction of your instruction. Allow their needs and interests to steer the course. In addition to lessons on conventions, don't forget to include lots of opportunities for students to examine writing samples and to discuss whether or not the qualities of good writing are present—whether the goals of the author have been successfully achieved. And although you never want to use your students' work as negative examples, do invite students to demonstrate good writing techniques during your instructional time.

In the previous chapter, I provided mini-lessons for the first month of the year: lessons that helped students become familiar with writer's workshop, and the trait of ideas. In October we'll take a peek at organization and some informational writing.

October

Focus: How Will I Organize My Writing?

When it comes to teaching primary students about writing and organization, we've tended to stick to the concept of a beginning, middle, and end. (Much to our amusement, our concrete thinkers don't hesitate to point to the top of the paper, the middle, and the bottom as if to say, "See? My writing has all three.") And yes, we teach our youngest writers to begin their pieces in a manner that will grab the reader (a skill presented this month) and to give their writing a satisfying ending, but I believe there is a greater knowledge we can share with primary students; that is, all writers *choose* the manner in which they organize their writing.

This seems likes such an obvious concept, but I do believe we inadvertently teach students the opposite. We seem to imply, as soon as we think students are ready, that there is one way to organize writing: the five-paragraph essay. And all organizational techniques, such as the hamburger paragraph, a technique no professional writer would *ever* limit himself or herself to using, seem to lead to this one pattern of organization.

Now, I have nothing against teaching students different organizational structures; the more structures they know, the more patterns they have to choose from. But what is essential is that they understand that most writers first ask: "What do I want to write about?" And then, once the topic has been decided: "How do I want to organize this piece?" They don't crowbar their writing into one "correct" form, but ask, "How can I best communicate this information? What would be the clearest, most helpful, most entertaining and, sometimes, most original way?"

The ideal writing program allows for a balance of discovery when it comes to organization and the teaching of different organizational structures. I suggest that with young children, we begin with discovery—helping them to recognize an author's organizational structure—and later teach them an organizational pattern or two (in this book we revisit organization in March). The mini-lessons at the beginning of October introduce primary students to the concept of organization, help them recognize organizational structures, and help them consider arranging information in useful ways. The mini-lessons at the end of the month ask students to pay attention to lively leads, beginnings that grab the reader and refuse to let go.

Remember, you are introducing students to the idea of organizational structures. I do not recommend that you show students a form and then ask that each and every one of them complete fill-in-the-blank sentences or apply the same structure to their writing. Organizing one's writing, like selecting an idea, is a skill that requires thinking, choice, and practice. When a young student runs up to you and says, "Look! I'm using the *Now and Ben* pattern," [from the book *Now and Ben: The Modern Inventions of Benjamin Franklin* by Gene Barretta (2006)], only my book is 'Me as a Baby, Me Now,'" you'll know that you've empowered your students to organize their writing from a genuine place of understanding.

Introducing Organization

On Hand: One of your own pieces, written without attention to organization and ready to be projected on the board or a screen.

Mini-Lesson: When ideas are presented willy-nilly, the audience has difficulty following our thinking or our story. Share one of your pieces with a lack of cohesive organization. Here is an example:

> Oh, no! I slid off the inner tube and swam back to shore as quickly as I could! When I finally turned to face the beach, my brothers looked like little action figures. Once, I sat on an inner tube and floated in the sea.

Ask your students, "Does this make sense?"

When they share their confusion, show them how you revised to give the piece an understandable beginning, middle, and end:

> Once, I sat on an inner tube and floated in the sea. When I finally turned around and faced the beach, my brothers looked like little action figures. Oh, no! I slid off the inner tube and swam back to shore as quickly as I could!

Talk about the importance of organization and tell students you'll be taking a closer look at how authors organize their work in the weeks to come.

Extension: When I share my writing, students inevitably ask, "Is this real?" I will often listen to their questions and return a day or two later with yet another revision:

> When I was eight, my family and I spent a day at the beach. I begged my younger brother to let me use his inner tube and finally, he gave in. I couldn't have been happier, sitting on that floating island, staring out to sea. I drifted with sailboats and seagulls. Suddenly, I heard someone calling. Spinning the tube around, I realized I had gone quite a distance. My brother looked like an action figure in a far away land! I slid off the inner tube and wildly swam toward shore. My arms tired and I had to let go of the inner tube, but I finally reached the beach. My brother was so relieved. He may have lost his inner tube, but he still had a sister!

How Did the Author Organize the Work?

On Hand: *Carmine: A Little More Red* by Melissa Sweet (2005) or any other mentor text that has an obvious organizational structure.

Mini-Lesson: This mentor text is a retelling of *Little Red Riding Hood* organized as an alphabet book. Read the book cover to cover for sheer enjoyment. In all likelihood students will recognize the fairy tale early on. When you've completed the story ask, "How did the author, Melissa Sweet, decide to organize her telling of *Little Red Riding Hood*?"

Suggest that students might want to try their hand at writing an ABC book.

Books with Clear, Predictable Structures

First the Egg by Laura Vaccaro
   Seeger (2007).
   Pattern: First the _____, then the _____
*Now and Ben: The Modern Inventions of
   Benjamin Franklin* by Gene Barretta (2006).
   Left-hand pages show invention we use
   now, right-hand pages tell how *Ben*
   conceived and developed the idea.
Fortunately by Remi Charlip (1994).
   Alternates *fortunately* and *unfortunately* to
   tell story.

That's Good! That's Bad! by Margery Cuyler
   (1991).
   Alternates good and bad news.
Previously by Allan Ahlberg (2008).
   Story told backwards.
The Great Blue House by Kate Banks (2005).
   Organized by season.
Things That Are Most in the World by Judi
   Barrett (1998).
   Repeated sentence: *The _____iest thing in
   the word is _____.*
Cookie's Week by Cindy Ward (1997).
   Organized by days of the week.

Extension: Begin a T-chart graphic organizer. On the left-hand side, write "Title." On the right-hand side, write "Organization." Read any of the books listed in the sidebar and ask students to point out the organizational structure.

Interactive Writing/Organization

On Hand: A mentor text that uses a clear organizational structure, such as those listed in the sidebar.

Mini-Lesson: After reading the text (you may wish to read the book earlier in the week to keep the mini-lesson brief), suggest writing an interactive story based on the text's organizational structure. For example, if you read *Cookie's Week* by Cindy Ward (1997), you might compose a classroom story based on the days of the week pattern:

> On Monday the students in Ms. Patterson's class forgot to take their chairs down. They sat on the floor!
> On Tuesday the students in Ms. Patterson's class forgot to change the calendar. They went to gym, but Mr. Walden wasn't there!

Extension: Try composing both fiction and informational texts using the organizational structure of favorite books with simple organizational patterns.

Making Organizational Choices

<u>On Hand:</u>   A number of picture books about animals written and/or illustrated by Steve Jenkins and Robin Page. You may have any combination of the following:

> *What Do You Do with a Tail Like This?* (2003)
> Facts are organized by body part.
> *I See a Kookaburra! Discovering Animal Habitats Around the World* (2005).
> Animals are organized by habitat.
> *Move* (2006).
> Animals are organized (in a chain) by the way they move.
> *Living Color* (2007).
> Animals are organized by color.
> *Dogs and Cats* (2007).
> This is a flip book: one half about cats, one half about dogs.
> *How Many Ways Can You Catch a Fly?* (2008).
> Facts are organized by prey.

<u>Mini-Lesson:</u>   Invite students to imagine that they are going to write a book about animal facts. Ask, "How might you organize your book?" List their responses. During pauses, suggest a new structure or two. This will often lead to new ideas and connections.

The number of responses your students provide will depend, of course, on their experience with literature and their practice in categorizing, but the following are just some of the answers they might provide. Animals can be organized by:

Alphabet	Habitat
Size	Color
What they eat	Species
Domesticated/wild	Nocturnal/diurnal
Hibernate or not	Number of legs
Fur, feathers, fins	Number of young

After students have generated a list of ways to organize animal facts, show them some of the ways Steve Jenkins has organized his work. Circle ideas in your list that Jenkins used and add new ones if necessary. Suggest that before students begin a new piece they ask themselves, "How do I want to organize my work?"

Extension: Suggest students search the nonfiction section of the school library to discover any other ways of organizing books about animal facts.

Model the Use of an Organizational Structure

On Hand: A selection of your own writing in which you've used a clear, simple organizational pattern. You might try one of the following:

- Ten Chores I Hate to Do (numbered list)
- Memories of My Pets (grouped by smallest to largest, species, or length of time with you, etc.)
- The Worst Day Ever (fortunately/unfortunately)

Mini-Lesson: Share your writing with students. Ask them to give you feedback using the same format as author's chair: pointing to what you have done well and then asking you questions for clarification or a discussion of author's craft. (See author's chair procedure on page 49 for more detail about the format.)

Extension: Begin a web of organizational structures. In the center, write "Organization." On the shoots radiating from the center, write organizational patterns such as "ABC," "Time Order," "Bed to Bed," "What's Good/What's Bad." From these circles, draw lines to book titles that follow the patterns. After reading books aloud, add the titles to your web in the appropriate places. Add organizational patterns as needed. Don't be afraid to make up your own names for these patterns.

Focus and Organization

On Hand: The list of "Things We Know About" (page 52), whiteboard, and marker.

Mini-Lesson: When writers take the time to consider the focus of their pieces, organization becomes much clearer. Choose one of the items from your student-generated list "Things We Know About" and ask students first to brainstorm possible focuses then to brainstorm potential ways of organizing the focused piece. Create a web on your whiteboard (Figure 5.1).

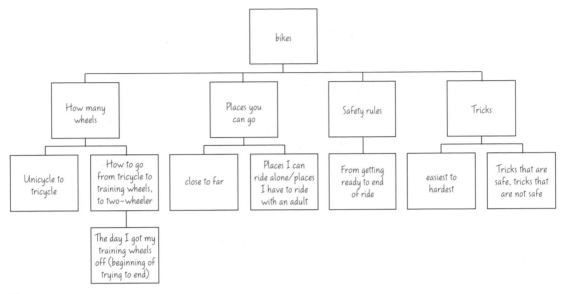

Figure 5.1
Finding a Focus

Extension: Collect a number of books about your chosen topic (in Figure 5.1, bicycles). Examine the books to determine the organizational forms.

Great Leads

On Hand: *Charlotte's Web* by E.B. White (1952).

Mini-Lesson: Share with the students that E.B. White wrote eight drafts of *Charlotte's Web*. (If you haven't introduced the concept of multiple drafts, here is a perfect opportunity.) He apparently had great difficulty with the beginning (as writers are apt to do), knowing that the beginning needs to do more than set the stage; it needs to instantly engage the reader. In draft B, his story began with the description of the barn—the text that opens Chapter 3 in the published draft. Tell students that you will read Mr. White's draft B beginning and then the published beginning and that you would like them to tell you which they believe is the better beginning.

From the start of Chapter 3, read:

The barn was very large. It was very old. It smelled of hay and it smelled of manure. It smelled of the perspiration of tired horses and the wonderful sweet breath of patient cows. It often had a sort of a peaceful smell—as though nothing bad could ever happen again in the world. It smelled of grain . . . [read to the end of the paragraph].

Then read from page 1:

"Where's Papa going with that ax?" said Fern to her mother as they were setting the table for breakfast.

"Out to the hog house," said Mrs. Arable. "Some pigs were born last night."

"I don't see why he needs an ax," continued Fern, who was only eight.

"Well," said her mother. "One of the pigs is a runt. It's very small and weak, and it will never amount to anything. So your father has decided to do away with it."

"Do away with it?" shrieked Fern. "You mean kill it? Just because it's smaller than the others?"

Figure 5.2
Who could resist reading a piece that begins: "A pig borrowed my box truck"?

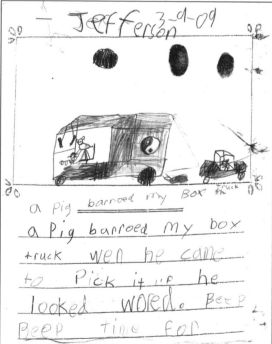

Discuss all of the reasons why the second beginning is much more effective than the first. During your talk you might point out some of the techniques authors have found effective:

- Begin with a question (and what a great question this one is!). When our brains consider a question, we read on to satisfy the longing for an answer.
- Begin with dialogue. No one ever listens to our mother's admonition to stop eavesdropping. We love to be privy to the conversations of others.
- Create a ticking clock. If Fern does not get out to that barn within minutes, a little piglet will die.

Extension: Examine beginnings in different books. Make a chart that records the lead and the techniques the authors used to capture the attention of readers.

Beginning Book Bags

On Hand: Approximately twenty books from your classroom library, sticky notes, five or six cloth book bags, duct tape, and a permanent marker.

Mini-Lesson: Tell students that you are going to read some of the leads from the books you gathered and that you would like them to look for similarities—for ways of categorizing the different leads. Students may begin to recognize some of the traditional ways we teach leads, recognizing that authors often use a question, dialogue, a sound, or description. Or they may come up with their own strategies for organizing the leads, such as the following:

- "Author talks to reader" (*Don't Let the Pigeon Drive the Bus!* by Mo Willems [2003], *No Laughing, No Smiling, No Giggling* by James Stevenson [2004])
- "-est beginnings," in which the author states a superlative: "Bella Lagrossi was the messiest monster in Booville" (*Boris and Bella* by Carolyn Crimi [2004]).
- "'It' leads": "It was in the summer of the year when the relatives came" (*The Relatives Came* by Cynthia Rylant [1985]) and "It was school picture day" (*School Picture Day* by Lynn Plourde [2002]).
- "Leads that tell when": "When Owen's granny heard he was a baby . . ." (*Banjo Granny* by Sarah Martin Busse and Jacqueline Briggs Martin [2006]), "Not so long ago, before she could even speak words . . ." (*Knuffle Bunny: A Cautionary Tale* by Mo Willems [2004]), "When I was younger it was plain to me . . ." (*A River of Words: The Story of William Carlos Williams* by Jen Bryant [2008]).

The excitement will grow as students begin to move the books around, deciding in which pile each belongs. Provide them with sticky notes to help them keep track. Some books will, simply because of your current pool, have no mates at all. Often students want to pull more books off the shelves; you may want to allow this to build upon their excitement, or you may want to suggest they continue to add to the bags or make new piles later. Once you've designated piles, place the books from each pile into a separate bag and use a strip of duct tape to label the bags with the appropriate category. Students can refer to the bags when trying to determine how to begin a piece, or they can take turns checking the bags out and reading the books with family members at home.

Extension: Suggest that students examine their own work and list the types of leads they've used.

One Day–Not!

On Hand: Sample writing that begins with "One day" to project on a screen or whiteboard.

Mini-Lesson: Many students, eager to plunge into writing, will begin with a tried and true "safety beginning." This is simply the manner in which they begin every piece. For the kindergarten student it might be "I like." First and second graders tend toward "One day," or "Once upon a time." To help students apply what they've been learning about beginnings, project a sample of writing (again, not from your class) with a safety lead. Suggest that students rewrite the beginning using a number of strategies they have identified. For example, take the lead, "One day my grandmother came over for breakfast" and rewrite it using one of the following techniques:

> Sound: *Crack! I had just broken the shell of my hardboiled egg when my grandmother came into the kitchen.*
> Question: *"What's for breakfast?" asked my grandmother as soon as she arrived.*
> —est beginning: *It was the silliest breakfast I'd ever had.*

Extension: Ask students to begin a new piece, but instead of writing one lead, have them write three different leads using three different strategies. They can share their possible leads with peers and then choose the one they believe is most engaging.

November

Focus: How Do I Write with Voice?

I have visited schools where well-intentioned teachers, believing that voice is a concept that is too difficult for primary children, have postponed the teaching of this trait until third grade. By now you know I oppose this thinking. Although the definition of voice can be hard to understand (granted, many professional writers disagree on the definition), voice can be easily recognized by primary students.

In fact, I believe five- to seven-year-olds come to school toting an enormous suitcase of voice, and it's our job as primary teachers to help them unpack it.

Unfortunately, we often want to take that suitcase and hide it in the supply closet. When we communicate in any way that our young students aren't ready to write, when we provide them with patterned or fill-in-the-blank sentences, when we ask them to copy sentences from the board, we are in a sense telling them that writing has nothing to do with their voices.

Instead, we should communicate from day one that our students not only have a lot to say but also have their own unique way of saying it. In other words, we should capture their natural voice on paper.

Introducing Voice

On Hand: Several picture books by Eric Carle and Jan Brett (or by other illustrators whose work is instantly recognizable).

Mini-Lesson: Introduce voice through art, beginning with picture books by Jan Brett. Show students several full-page spreads and ask them what they notice about her art. Here are some of the most common answers:

- She incorporates lots of details.
- Her work is framed—usually by borders.
- She often paints animals and seems drawn to nature.
- She provides little "windows"—glimpses of what has happened and what will happen.

Validate student responses by telling them that Jan Brett has a very distinctive artistic *voice*. That's what makes her work so instantly recognizable.

Then show them the work of Eric Carle and ask, "What can you tell me about his voice?" Students might suggest:

- His work is fanciful (pretend)—more imaginary than realistic.
- His shapes are large, bright, bold.
- He does not include a realistic background, though he sometimes fills the page with colorful shapes.
- You can see his brush strokes in some of his work.

Eric Carle has an equally distinctive voice, but one that's very different from Jan Brett's. Test students by holding up artwork by one of these two illustrators and asking, "Whose work is this?" You'll find that they don't hesitate to identify the artist.

Tell students that these illustrators have their own artistic voice and that they have a distinct writer's voice. Explain that if you are a bubbly person, chances are your writing voice is bubbly too. Or perhaps you're a fairly serious person, in which case your writing voice might be serious. Voices can be humorous, angry, laid-back—and there is a place in the writing world for all these voices.

Invite students to write with attention to voice and show their unique style. Tell them: "Your voice is as unique as your thumbprint. Put your thumbprint on your work today."

Extension: In the picture book *Why Did the Chicken Cross the Road?* by Jon Agee et al. (2006), fourteen artists offer a punch line to the age-old riddle, giving us the perfect opportunity to examine different artistic responses to the very same subject. Read the book to students and ask them to provide adjectives, from sweet to silly, to describe the tone of the visuals. Reinforce the idea that each illustrator used his or her own unique voice.

Listening for Voice

On Hand: *I Stink* by Kate McMullen (2002) or any other picture books that demonstrate clear voice, both to the ear and to the eye (in the font). (See the sidebar for more recommendations on books that play with font.)

Mini-Lesson: Read *I Stink* with much expression. After reading, show students that the author not only wrote with a fun, rowdy, He-Man voice, she also showed voice in the font. Allow students to make observations of the print. Ask, "What did the author and the book designer do with the print?" (Possible responses: "At times it's bold," "It stretches," "It bounces up and down.") Ask, "Why do you think they made these choices?" Encourage students to read the words in unusual fonts with you and to use their voices in these very distinct ways.

 The following books demonstrate voice in both the language and in the font design. What a concrete way to help our youngest learners grow in their understanding of voice!

A Visitor for Bear by Bonny Becker (2008).
Big Bad Bunny by Franny Billingsley (2008).
Henry and the Buckaneer Bunnies by Carolyn Crimi (2005).
Holly's Red Boots by Francesca Chessa (2008).
How to Be a Good Dog by Gail Page (2006).

Extension: Suggest that students play with their own print to emphasize their voices.

Feelings Included

On Hand: An expressive phrase from a story you've read, such as "Where is all this going to end?" from *Brave Charlotte* by Anu Stohner (2005).

Mini-Lesson: Ask students to take turns saying the phrase using the following voices: angry, sad, silly, whiny, happy, frustrated, serious, confused, and so on.

    Tell students that adding feelings to writing often adds heaps of voice. Remind them that the words around the phrase—the details the author includes—helps us to know how to read a phrase and how the character (or in some cases the author) is feeling.

Extension: Invite students who have done a good job in expressing feeling in their writing to coteach the mini-lesson with you the next day.

Voice in Informational Texts

On Hand: *Chameleon, Chameleon* by Joy Cowley (2005) or another informational text that demonstrates lively voice.

Mini-Lesson: Read the story cover to cover for the pure enjoyment of the language and suspense. When the book is completed, reread it (this is a very short text; if you've chosen a longer text, you might want to reread it during the next day's mini-lesson). When you reread the book, encourage the students to put their thumbs up whenever they recognize strong voice. Stop and discuss the techniques the author used, such as the following:

- Fabulous word choice: *peaceful, juicy, creeps*
- Interjections: "No food! No food!" "Zap!" "Chew, chew, gulp!"
- The way the author draws sentences out to create suspense: "Slowly the chameleon climbs down the tree, step . . . by step . . . by step. He stops."
- Using questions: "Is something hiding there?"

Help students to understand that *all* writing, whether it is a story or an informational book or article, should be written with voice.

Extension: Leave a stack of sticky notes in your classroom library on the day of the mini-lesson. Invite students to search for voice in your library's informational texts. Have them mark pages that demonstrate voice. Present those passages at the next day's mini-lesson and allow students the opportunity to tell why they chose these particular places in the text.

Recognizing Voice

On Hand: One personal story written two ways: without voice and with voice. Write the passages on chart paper or project the stories on a screen for easy viewing.

Mini-Lesson: Tell students that you have written the same story in two ways. Read the first narrative, which might be similar to this one:

> There was mold growing in a container in my refrigerator. The food was spoiled, so I threw it out.

Now share the second:

> I knew it was in there, somewhere. I had purchased a carton of my favorite banana vanilla yogurt, and if I wasn't mistaken, I still had

some left. Yes! I thought as I spotted it in the back. I opened the lid, eager to dive in, and spotted one of my worst enemies: refrigerator mold. Not only was it quicker at gobbling up my favorite foods than I was, but it clung to the sides of each container, refusing to be washed down the sink without a fight. I prepared myself for battle—and to gag.

Ask, "Which of these two passages has more voice?" Even the youngest of students will be able to identify the second. We may not be able to easily *define* voice, but we all recognize it when we see it.

Now ask, "How did I present more voice in the second passage?" Students will offer a variety of observations, which may include:

- You used more details. (The details an author chooses show his or her particular view of the world, and thus reveals voice.)
- The use of "Yes!" (This conveys enthusiasm and energy, both qualities of voice.)
- You said, "spotted one of my worst enemies." (We experience voice when the author presents an idea uniquely.)
- You used more lively verbs: *purchased, spotted, dive, gobbling, clung, gag.*
- The first one sounded like this: blah, blah, blah . . . The second one was more ooh! ooh! ooh!

Extension: Take a passage (perhaps one from a favorite book) that has lots of voice and, with the students, reduce it to a few lines without voice.

Conferencing to Explore Voice

Conferencing with students can be an incredibly effective way to help students write with more voice. I often begin the conference by saying, "Please read your piece to me, and as you read, I'm going to listen for places where your unique voice comes through." When the child has finished reading, I might point to the following:

* Interesting use of language ("That sounds just like you!")
* Fabulous word choice
* Inclusion of feelings
* Strong sensory details
* Use of interjections or dialogue
* Effective use of repetition

I am reinforcing the writer's craft, helping the student understand that all of these skills can help voice shine through. If the student's piece lacks any voice I might say, "Let's pick one phrase that we can work with to help you bring more voice to this piece." When we've revised that section, I will try to help the student understand exactly why the change brought voice so he or she can use the technique in his or her next piece.

What Did You Learn About the Writer?

On Hand: Samples of student writing, one with voice, another without.

Mini-Lesson: Project a sample of writing that has little voice. For example:

> Tomorrow is my birthday.
> I am turning seven.
> I am having a carnival party.

Ask, "What do you know about this writer that you didn't learn from the words?" Guide students to understand that when there is little voice, we don't learn about the author. Then project a piece that has more voice, such as the piece in Figure 5.3.

Figure 5.3
"I Have a Boo-Boo"

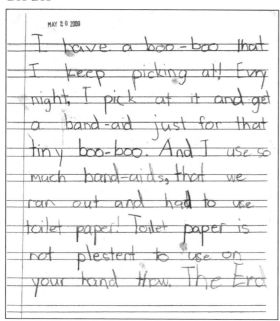

MAY 2 0 2009

I have a boo-boo that I keep picking at! Evry night, I pick at it and get a band-aid just for that tiny boo-boo. And I use so much band-aids, that we ran out and had to use toilet paper! Toilet paper is not plestent to use on your hand thow. The End

Ask, "What can you tell me about this writer?" Students will likely come up with a range of responses, many making personal connections:

"She has a hard time breaking a habit—like me."
"She knows she doesn't need that many Band-Aids because she calls the cut tiny."
"She's funny. She has a good sense of humor."
"She doesn't like having to use toilet paper."

Tell students that when they write with voice, readers are better able to understand their meaning and feel a connection to the author.

Extension: Have students examine their own writing for voice. Which sentence(s) do they think provides the reader with added information?

Voice T-Chart

On Hand: The book *Rain Romp* by Jane Kurtz (2002) or any other book with lots of voice, and a whiteboard.

Mini-Lesson: Draw a T-chart on your board. Label the left column "Examples of Voice"; label the right column "How Author Creates Voice" (see Figure 5.4). Reread the book and ask students to stop you when they hear a phrase that brings voice to the piece. Record the phrase on the right-hand side of the chart. Then ask, "What did the author do that made this sentence stand out?" This exercise is entirely open-ended. There is no right or wrong answer when it comes to voice, but the window into your students' thinking will be very illuminating.

Figure 5.4
Voice T-Chart

Examples of voice:	How author does it:
"I don't feel shiny."	unique way of saying something
"Dad hums a snazzy jazzy tune."	writing shows enthusiasm
"No way," I say. "Noooo way."	Demonstrates attitude.
"The rain agrees with me."	New way of looking at something.

Second Person Point of View

On Hand: A book written in second person (addressing the reader as *you*), such as *Time of Wonder* by Robert McCloskey (1957)

Mini-Lesson: Read the story aloud. Many will simply enjoy the immediacy of second person:

The rain comes closer and closer.
Now you hear a million splashes.
Now you even see the drops
on the water . . .
on the age-old rocky point . . .
on the bayberry . . .
on the grass . . .
now take a breath-
IT'S RAINING ON YOU!

Some of your students, however, will grab onto this voice and run with it. What fun your students will have addressing the reader in second person. Oh, what voice those pieces will have!

December

Focus: How Do I Choose the Very Best Word?

Focusing on word choice is a favorite activity for many primary teachers, and I can certainly understand why. After examining qualities that seem as wide and expansive as a Midwestern sky (focus, organization, voice), exploring the just-right word seems downright indulgent. Not to mention rewarding. Attention to the specificity and vitality of words can transform a predictable, blah piece into one that pulses with energy.

Writers are artists and words are their tools. What we want most to convey to primary students is that writers choose their words *carefully*. We want the most accurate word, the most vivid word, and sometimes the most entertaining word.

Do you remember a first day of school when you either arrived with a cache of new supplies or your teacher gave you supplies—perhaps even a box of unopened crayons? Do you remember the joy of seeing that array of colors? The perfectly

Word Banks

Many primary teachers are attracted to individual student dictionaries: books with frequently spelled words under each letter and spaces for students to add their own. If you wish to purchase these for your students, I'd recommend waiting until the second half of the year to pass them out. Students can easily build an overdependence on the books and spend much of their writing time searching for words and only writing those words that are listed. Once students have confidence in their ability to write *any* word—whether they can spell it or not—and when they demonstrate an understanding that it's the message that matters most, then they are ready for word banks.

sharpened points? I want to create that kind of excitement at the beginning of this month. I want students to feels as if I've just handed them a big box of juicy, colorful words. Let the creating begin!

Modeling Choice

On Hand: A large sheet of construction paper and markers or crayons.

Mini-Lesson: Choose someone to whom you (not necessarily your class) would like to send a note. It might be a thank-you note, a birthday card, or a get-well card. Introduce your task to students and then fold the construction paper in two. Use a black marker to draw the outline of an appropriate picture on the front. Now select colors for your illustration and as you do, tell students why you are choosing them. For example, you might say: "Let's see, I want to choose the just-right colors. My friend isn't feeling well and I want to cheer her up, so I am choosing this bright pink for the teapot. Pink always makes me feel happier. Oh, and yellow—yellow reminds me of the sun, which is bright and cheerful and warm. I'll make the tablecloth yellow."

Then open the card and tell students that you want to write a note to your friend, but that you want to choose your words as carefully as you chose the colors for the picture on the front. As you write the note, think out loud to allow students to hear your decisions around word choice: "Instead of writing 'I hope you feel better soon,' I am going to choose words that are more specific and more fun. I am going to write, 'Sorry to hear the nasty flu is visiting your house. I'm sending cups of love.'"

Tell students that writers are always searching for the very best way to say something.

Extension: If you are indeed doing this lesson in December, take the traditional "happy holidays" and see if your students can't come up with some other choices for "happy": *cheerful, song-full, peaceful, unforgettable, surprising, loving, yummy.* If your students have difficulty coming up with adjectives, ask them to tell you about their favorite holiday memories. Then give the memory an adjective. This is a great way to teach vocabulary in context.

Striking Words and Phrases

On Hand: Any picture book with lively, playful language, such as *And Here's to You* by David Eliot (2004)

Mini-Lesson: Read the book to your students, then reread it. On the second reading, ask students to stop you when they hear a word or phrase that really stands out. Record the language on chart paper labeled "Words We Admire" and post the chart on the wall. Add to your list whenever you and students come across a particularly stunning word or phrase.

Extension: Do what teacher Mindy Burns does to get her students collecting interesting vocabulary. She reads *Fancy Nancy* by Jane O'Connor (2005) and then creates a "Fancy Words" bulletin board. All year long, students post dazzling words on the board and frequently incorporate the vocabulary in their writing.

Collecting Words

On Hand: *Max's Words* by Kate Banks (2006), index cards with a single hole punched in the corner (five to ten for each student), and one loose-leaf ring for each student. Optional: Old magazines, glue sticks, and scissors.

Mini-Lesson: After reading *Max's Words*, a story about a boy who decided to collect words, provide each student with ten index cards bound on a ring and invite them to begin their own word collections. Suggest that they write words they particularly love or are enchanted by on the cards. You might want to encourage them to cut words from magazines as Max did and glue them onto their cards. Encourage the students to use their cards as a resource when writing.

Extension: What are your favorite words? Have students interview family members to find answers to this question. Invite students to share the responses during the mini-lesson on the next day.

Sound Words

On Hand: *Mouse's First Snow* by Lauren Thompson (2005) or other text that uses onomatopoeia. Optional: chart paper or a whiteboard.

Mini-Lesson: When it comes to selecting dazzling words—particularly ones that deliver more voice—onomatopoeia is one of the simplest and most effective strategies for primary students. After reading the story once for pleasure, I return to the text and point out the sound words that Lauren Thompson has included (*Woosh, Swoosh! Pliff, Ploof!*) and ask, "How do these words make you feel?" Guide students to understand that sounds help the reader feel as if he or she were there in the story experiencing everything that Mouse is experiencing.

Invite students to add sound words to their writing.

Other Recommended Titles with Onomatopoeia

Aunt Nancy and Old Man Trouble by Phyllis Root (1996).
Avalanche Annie: A Not-So-Tall Tale by Lisa Wheeler (2003).
Book, Book, Book! by Deborah Brus (2001).
Officer Buckle and Gloria by Peggy Rathman (1995).
One Frog Sang by Shirley Parenteau (2007).
Snow Sounds: An Onomatopoeic Story by David A. Johnson (2006).
The Little Mouse, the Red Ripe Strawberry, and the Big Hungry Bear by Don and Audrey Wood (1994).

Extension: Model the use of the editor's caret. (What I love about Thompson's text is that the onomatopoeia is set off, almost as if these words were added in a revision.) Write a sentence without a sound, and then show the students how the caret (which they no doubt picture as a carrot tip) helps a writer go back and add words to the sentence:

> rah, rah, rah,
>
> It was so cold this morning that when I turned the key,^ my car wouldn't start!

More Fun with Onomatopoeia

On Hand: *Snow Music* by Lynne Rae Perkins (2003)

Mini-Lesson: Read *Snow Music*. Take some time to compare this book with *Mouse's First Snow* by Lauren Thompson (2005). Guide students to understand that the words Thompson chose create a lively, carefree romp, whereas the words Perkins selected on some pages ("peth, peth, peth") create a more hushed, whispery quality.

Extension: Read *Inside Mouse, Outside Mouse* by Lindsay Barrett George (2004), which is a fabulous addition to any primary classroom. The pages compare the lives of two mice with brief, repetitive text that contains many high-frequency words. (Students are eager to read this story independently.) Point out that *Inside Mouse, Outside Mouse* does not have sound words. Invite students to come up with sound words to accompany the text on each page. (No need to record the words unless you wish. Students will benefit from the practice of thinking about actions and the sounds they make.)

Vigorous Verbs

On Hand: *To Root to Toot to Parachute: What Is a Verb?* by Brian P. Cleary (2001), slips of paper with verbs from the book written on them (be careful to choose actions that can be acted out in your meeting area), chart paper, and a marker.

Mini-Lesson: Choosing specific and visual verbs can transform writing. Look at the difference a verb makes to the sentence *She went into the store*:

> She raced into the store.
> She trudged into the store.
> She snuck into the store.
> She slipped into the store.

When primary students write with lively, specific verbs, their compositions pop. If you haven't introduced actions words, consider doing so with Brian Cleary's fun celebration of verbs. After reading this text, provide each of your students with a slip of paper and invite them to perform a charade of the action printed on the paper. As students guess what the action is, record their responses. When the activity is over, you'll have a "verb wall" to post in the room for reference.

Extension: Read *Mammoths on the Move* by Lisa Wheeler (2006), which is packed with lively verbs for students to enact: "Stepping, Stomping/Marching, Tromping/ Watch out Wooly Mammoths!"

"Sun Cartwheels Slowly Up the Sky"

On Hand: *Water Hole Waiting* by Jane and Christopher Kurtz (2002) or other mentor text with strong, unique verbs, whiteboard or chart paper; markers; and a sample of writing with blah verbs.

Mini-Lesson: Read the picture book, pausing to let students visualize some of the strong verbs. For example, if reading *Water Hole Waiting*, you might stop at, "Sun cartwheels slowly up the sky, herding hippopotami." Discuss how the Kurtzes chose verbs that are unexpected but allow the reader to see the action clearly.

Now project writing that is lacking in specific, lively verbs. Your sample might be something like the following:

> Yesterday I went to the park. First I went on the swings. Then my brother and I went on the seesaw. My brother got off too quickly and I went down.

After a brief discussion, circle the occurrences of the word *went*. Ask students to suggest more vivid verbs to use instead. When there is a lull in the brainstorm, wait. In all likelihood students will come up with the dazzling verbs after the more obvious ones have been recorded. Initially students might come up with "Then my brother and I rode the seesaw," but with a little time and exploration, students may offer verbs such as *balanced, teetered, flew,* or even *elevatored* or *up-downed*. Primary students may not have a large vocabulary to draw from, but they do have a willingness to play with words and to see things from a fresh perspective.

Extension: Have students circle the action words in their own writing. Invite them to choose three words they circled and brainstorm a list of alternative verbs. Then have them choose the very best words from the lists.

January

Focus: How Do I Make My Writing Flow?

Fluent writing is a delight to hear read aloud. There is a flow from sentence to sentence that engages the reader and invites him or her to come along. Fluent writers use a variety of sentence beginnings and sentence lengths, but they don't do this by focusing on grammar or by counting the number of words. They do this by ear.

Audio books are a wonderful way to keep all of your kids listening to fine writing on regular basis. I recommend purchasing MP3 players for students for use during the school day and at home. They need not be iPods. In fact, it is still easier to download books on the less expensive players. Many public libraries subscribe to a service that allows free downloads.

Primary writers who have been read to, or who themselves are avid readers, will be the first to write fluently. They are the ones who have had experience with the pacing of fine writing. They've heard writers use repetition for interest. They've learned that several long sentences followed by a halting short sentence or sentence fragment makes a point or provides punch. These students may not be able to articulate these sophisticated techniques, but they're beginning to execute them just the same.

Therefore the most important thing we can do to support writing fluency is to read aloud. Including daily read-aloud time is essential. The more students listen to exceptional writing, the more fluent their writing will become.

A Sweet-Sounding Train

On Hand: Two samples of your own writing, one that lacks fluency and one that sings. (Write each sentence on a separate line so beginnings can be compared.)

Mini-Lesson: Project the writing sample that lacks fluency. Here is my example:

> I have two little dogs.
> They're named Kenzie and Hattie.
> They are fun to walk.
> They like to eat treats.

Tell students that this first attempt at writing chugs along like a slow-moving train—one that's about to break down. Have students bend their arms at the elbow and, moving them simultaneously, imitate that old, nearly broken-down train: "Chug . . . chug . . . chug . . ." Show them that this writing "chugs" because almost every sentence begins with the same word and all of the sentences are the same length. (Have students count the words in the sentence with you.)

Now project your second piece of writing. Here is mine:

I have two little dogs name Kenzie and Hattie.
They're fun to walk in the park.
After they've zipped around, saying hello to all the other dogs, they
    bounce back to me for a treat.

Ask students, "Which of these pieces sounds better to the ear?" Guide them to understand that the varied beginnings and sentence lengths help to make the second piece more pleasant sounding. When writing is fluent, tell them, it sounds like a steady-moving train. Have them imitate the melodious sounds of a smooth-running train: "Clickerty, clickerty, clack, clickerkty, clickerty, clack . . . " or even, "Cha-ch-sh, Cha-ch-sh, Cha-ch-sh . . ."

Suggest they try to write sentences that flow like a sweet-sounding train.

Extension: Read a book with train sound effects, such as *The Train Goes . . .* by William Bee (2007). Discuss the fluency of this text:

Here is the school class off on a trip,
and the children yell,
'Please, sir, please, ma'am . . . are we there yet?'

Admiring Fluent Writing

On Hand: A lyrical picture book, such as *The Night Is Singing* by Jacqueline Davies (2006), and the text from a favorite page written on chart paper or prepared to project on a screen or whiteboard.

Mini-Lesson: After reading the picture book from beginning to end, show students the text from a page or two. Read the pages aloud and invite students to tap the rhythm using their hands or feet.

Then ask them to make observations about the print. This is an open-ended exercise, so validate all responses. Students might notice the following:

- Some words rhyme.
- Some sentences are long: "The house is singing lullabies."
  And some sentences are short: "Up you go." There are even one word sentences: "Sleepy?"

- There are dashes between some words: "tell-the-timing,"
  "streak-and-fly." (Let students know that authors often like to
  create a string of words, like a beaded necklace.)
- Jacqueline Davies sometimes begins her stanzas with an
  action word: "Hear the hissing," or "Watch them go."

Encourage students to create works that flow like the words on these
pages.

Extension: Suggest that students try tapping the rhythm of their own work. Do
they like the way it sounds? What changes might they make?

Sentence Stretching

On Hand: Chart paper or board, marker, and if possible an individual whiteboard or clipboard for each student.

Mini-Lesson: Write the following sentence on the board: *I went for a walk*. Tell students that you would like them to imagine themselves on a walk. Tell
them that you are going to ask a series of questions and that they
should write down one or two words on their own board to answer the
question. (If you teach kindergarten, of if you think your students will
need more assistance, conduct this lesson as a whole-group interactive
writing activity.) Ask:

- When did you walk?
- Who did you walk with?
- Where did you go?
- What did you see?
- Why did you go on the walk?

Now invite students to rewrite the initial sentence using as many
of their answers as they wish. Tell them it's okay to leave one or two of
the answers out. Encourage students to share their responses, which
may resemble this sentence:

> Yesterday I went walking with my mother down by the river
> to look for animal tracks, but we didn't see any.

Stretching sentences in this way gives students a new confidence
and pride in their ability to construct lovely phrases.

Extension: Make a list titled "Words That Tell When" on chart paper and post it for students to refer to when looking for varied sentence beginnings. Your chart might include: *yesterday, today, tomorrow, after, before, earlier, on* (day of week), *in* (month), *when, long ago, back.* Students will no doubt want to keep adding to this list as they discover new ways of beginning sentences.

Song Writing

On Hand: *Astro Bunnies* by Christine Loomis (2001) or any other picture book based on a familiar song structure, a whiteboard or chart paper, and a marker.

Mini-Lesson: Read the book once just as you would any other picture book, then read it again. On the second read, point out to students that the author, Christine Loomis, wrote the words to the tune of "Twinkle Twinkle Little Star." Sing a page or two:

> It's always wonderful when you can extend students' understanding of craft by sharing an author's unique process. For example, Jacqueline Davies reports that when writing *The Night Is Singing* (2006), a rhythm just came to her and she wrote according to the sound she heard in her head: da-da-DA-da, da-da-DA-da, da-da-DA-da, da-da-DA. You can find information about author's process online, either by visiting authors' Web sites or reading interviews on blogs. Simply search by an author's name.

Astro bunnies
See a star
Think they'd like to
Go that far

Now choose a classroom topic (jobs, an upcoming event, or writer's workshop, for example) and compose your own song to the tune of "Twinkle, Twinkle":

Writer's Workshop
Every day
We compose
With words we play

Working with different language structures helps students break out of too-familiar sentence patterns and write with more fluency. Invite students to borrow the rhythm when composing.

Extension: Investigate picture book adaptations of the song "The Wheels on the Bus." You might include *The Seals on the Bus* by Lenny Hort (2000) and *Library Doors* by Toni Buzzeo (2008).

Writing with Refrains

On Hand: *The Boy Who Cried Wolf* by B.G. Hennessy (2006) or any other picture book that has a repetitive language.

Mini-Lesson: Read the story twice, and on the second reading, invite students to chime in on the repeating refrain. Then begin a chart of familiar books that have a refrain. Write "Title" on the left, and "Refrain" on the right. For example, your chart might look like the one in Figure 5.5.

Figure 5.5
Recognizing and
Recording
Refrains

Title	Refrain
The Boy Who Cried Wolf by B.G. Hennessy	Munch, munch, munch Baaaaa . . . . No wolves in the . . .
The Gingerbread Man by Karen Schmidt	Run, run as fast as you can . . .
Who Hops? by Katie Davis	No they don't!
A Visitor For Bear by Bonny Becker	Small and gray and bright-eyed
Trashy Town by Andrea Zimmerman	Dump it in, smash it down, drive around the Trashy Town!
School Picture Day by Lynn Plourde	fidgeting, fiddling, fuddling, and foopling

While focusing on refrains, you might want to discuss the difference between intended repetition and overuse of familiar sentence patterns. Writers use repetition to create a poetic rhythm:

> *"Not I," said the Duck.*
> *"Not I," said the Cat.*
> *"Not I," said the Dog.*
> *"Then I will," said the Little Red Hen. And she did.*

Suggest that students read their work aloud to see if the repetition they use creates the sounds of poetry or whether it simply bores the reader.

Extension: Write the text of familiar chants and rhymes on chart paper for choral readings. For example, you might use the following:

<u>Three Little Monkeys</u>
Three little monkeys swinging from a tree,
Teasing Mr. Alligator, "Can't catch me!"
Along came Mr. Alligator slowly as can be
Then . . . SNAP!
Two little monkeys swinging from a tree,
Teasing Mr. Alligator, "Can't catch me!"
Along came Mr. Alligator slowly as can be
Then . . . SNAP!
One little monkey swinging from a tree,
Teasing Mr. Alligator, "Can't catch me!"
Along came Mr. Alligator slowly as can be
Then . . . SNAP!

Reader's Theater

On Hand: A copy of a reader's theater script for each student who will be reading.

Note: Scripts can be found on the Internet or in resource books such as *Once Upon a Time: Using Storytelling, Creative Drama, and Reader's Theater with Children in Grades PreK–6* by Judy Freeman (2007) and *Read! Perform! Learn! 2: 10 Reader's Theater Programs for Literacy Enhancement* by Toni Buzzeo (2007). Some authors, such as Katie Davis (*Mabel the Tooth Fairy and How She Got Her Job* [2003]), post scripts of their books online. You can also create your own script using classic fairy tales.

Mini-Lesson: Have students perform a story for classmates. With reader's theater (also known as book-in-hand theater) students do not memorize lines, but read them aloud. Nevertheless, a rehearsal or two is recommended, as a practiced performance will increase enjoyment for both the audience and the readers. Encourage students to become the characters by using facial expressions, altered voices, and gestures. In other words, invite them to ham it up. Not only does reader's theater help improve students' writing fluency, it also aids in reading fluency.

Extension: Invite students to write their own scripts (original or based on published texts) to be performed with a classmate. Suggest they divide a sheet of paper in half and write each person's dialogue on one side. Then tear the sheet down the middle so the two may hold their parts as they perform. (You may want to make a copy for students' folders before the tear.)

Poetry Slam

On Hand: *Barnyard Slam* by Dian Curtis Regan (2009).

Mini-Lesson: After reading *Barnyard Slam*, suggest students plan a poetry reading of their own. Invite families, another class, or school personnel to come and hear original student poems or favorite poems written by others. Push the desks together to create cafe tables and cover them with cloths. Suggest students wear bandanas—just like the animal poets in the story! Encourage them to practice reading their poems aloud and to concentrate on expression. Invite the audience to snap their fingers to show their appreciation of poems.

February

Focus: How Do I Include Quality Details?

In September you helped students focus their topics and include detail, and now the spiral has circled back to this topic. Barry Lane implores us to "explode the moment" (1999, 97). Lucy Calkins teaches us to zoom in on our small seed ideas (1994, 25) Learning to slow down time, to include details that go beyond the obvious or the general—this is the skill that, perhaps, has the greatest impact on writing. Why? Because doing so also increases voice, attention to word choice, and sentence fluency.

　　Each of us has a unique perspective on the world. By inevitably selecting some details over others, we not only help the reader to imagine—to fall into the work—we also help them to feel connected to the writer. That is, to us.

Focusing on the Details

On Hand: A wordless picture book, such as *Flotsam* by David Wiesner (2006).

Mini-Lesson:　Begin telling this story by making up narration to go with the pictures, and model attention to the illustration details on each page. Point out that instead of saying "The boy saw a camera," you will say, "Now soaking wet, with seaweed caught between his toes, the boy noticed a camera—also covered in seaweed—lying in the sand."

　　After you have demonstrated this manner of telling for a few pages, invite individuals to come up and tell what happens next. Reinforce their ability to extract details from the illustrations and weave them into the telling.

Extension:　Remind students that drawing is an excellent form of prewriting. Suggest they try drawing the next scene of their work to discover details they might like to use in their writing.

Another Look at Sensory Details

On Hand:　*The Dirty Cowboy* by Amy Timberlake (2003) or any other picture book that uses strong sensory language.

Mini-Lesson:　Read the story once, then prepare to reread the first page. Ask students to close their eyes and see if the writing causes them to feel as if they, too, are right there with the main character:

> *At the end of two fence lines and right at the rock called The Praying Iguana lived a cowboy in a tin-roofed shack.*
> *Every morning, he'd call his dog, mount his horse, and spend the day tracking stray longhorn cattle on the New Mexico range.*
> *Every evening, he'd stoke his fire and fry up some bacon, beans, and potatoes while whistling "The Streets of Laredo."*

　　Share one of your reactions: "I could feel the warmth of that campfire," and invite students to do the same: "I could smell the bacon cooking," "I could hear the whistling," and so on.

　　Remind students that by selecting details that engage all of our senses, we help readers imagine themselves in the place of the writer or main character. Suggest students use an editing pencil to circle the sensory words in their own writing.

Extension:　Invite students to search for passages in their reading that allow readers to imagine a sound, touch, smell, or taste.

Show, Don't Tell

On Hand: Whiteboard or chart paper.

Mini-Lesson: Remind students, "The job of the writer is to create a movie in the mind of a reader." Writers often do this by refraining from simply telling us how things are, but showing us instead. Write a simple telling sentence such as the one Molly Hogan wrote in Figure 5.6: "The room was very messy." Now invite students to collaborate in writing a paragraph that shows rather than tells the reader just what messy means.

Figure 5.6
Using Detail to
Create a Visual
Image

> * <u>Telling</u> *
> The room was very messy.
>
> * <u>Showing</u> *
> Coffee grounds, orange peels and bright, crumpled wrappers spilled out of the trash can and littered the floor. A brown, moldy banana stuck to the blanket of the bed. A whiteboard and markers hid halfway under the bed. Uncapped permanent markers dried out in a dusty corner. In the center of the room lay a broken guitar. Inside the guitar was a mouse nest filled with crumbs and nibbles of cheese.

<u>Extension:</u> Read *Mrs. McBloom, Clean Up Your Classroom* by Kelly Dipucchio (2005). Project an illustration of Mrs. McBloom's amazing mess. With students, write a paragraph or two that describes her unique chaos.

Imagine That

<u>On Hand:</u> *Love the Baby* by Stephen L. Layne (2007) or any other book that shows, through actions, a character's emotions.

<u>Mini-Lesson:</u> Read text from the book that demonstrates how a character is feeling through action. For example, from *Love the Baby* you might read: "So I built a tower for Baby . . . and then I knocked it down!" Ask, "How is this big brother feeling in this moment?" After students have provided responses, point out that the author did not use words such as *mad, angry, frustrated,* or *jealous*. But we, the readers, know that this is how the brother is feeling because of his actions. The details the author selected *show* us how the character is feeling.

Next, ask students to imagine they have just learned that they won the school art contest. Say, "Your picture will be framed and hung in the front hall. It will be the first piece of art seen as we come into the building. How do you react?"

Invite volunteers to come up and demonstrate a reaction. Invite others to provide the words that show through actions how the student is feeling. Remind them to stay away from words that tell, such as *happy, excited,* and *thrilled*:

Teacher: Kara just learned that she won the school art contest.
Student response: She jumped into the air and shouted, "Yes!"

You might want students to act out several scenarios. Here are other suggestions:

- Your babysitter has just accused you of doing something you didn't do. You say, "But . . ." She interrupts you and tells you to go to your room. How do you exit?
- A hurricane blows over a favorite tree—one that you've climbed countless times, the one where you built your tree fort. How do you react?

Suggest that students provide details to show how they or their main characters are feeling through actions.

Extension: Provide students with sentences that tell how a character feels and invite them to rewrite the sentences to show how a character feels. Have them share their rewrites at the next day's morning meeting.

Tiny Stitches

On Hand: *I Could Do That: Esther Morris Gets Women the Vote* by Linda Arms White (2005), whiteboard or chart paper, and a marker.

Mini-Lesson: After reading *I Could Do That*, tell students that you admire the author's ability to slow time down, to show us all of the actions that occur while accomplishing a small task. Point out that Linda Arms White could have simply written, "Esther learned to sew by watching her mother." But instead she wrote:

> *When Esther was eight, she watched her mother sew a fine seam. The needle pulled thread in and out, in and out, tracking tiny even stitches across the fabric. Esther felt her hands mimicking her mother's. "I could do that," she said. And she did.*

Now model writing a paragraph about a simple task that you do, but break it down into smaller actions. For example, you might write about the manner in which you make your bed, feed the dog, or eat an ear of corn. Chances are students will want to tell you about the way in which they do these routines. We connect in the sharing of details.

Extension: Ask students to write about a simple task, such as brushing their teeth. Tell them they must slow the writing down to fill an entire page. Once students have practiced unpacking a moment in this way, they will be able to apply the skill to their own writing.

Quality Details in Expository Writing

On Hand: *Ice Bear: In the Steps of the Polar Bear* by Nicola Davies (2005).

Mini-Lesson: Tell students that details help to make writing more interesting. Write this sentence on the board: "Polar bears stay warm when it's cold outside." Tell students that this sentence, without any quality details, is a "snoozer"—the kind of writing that lulls us to sleep. Then read to them from Davies's book:

> *No frost can steal Polar Bear's heat. It has a double coat: one of fat, four fingers deep, and one of fur which has an extra trick for beating cold. Its hairs aren't really white, but hollow, filled with air, to stop the warmth escaping, and underneath, the skin is black to soak up heat.*

 Two other exemplary nonfiction texts model the use of quality details:

Stars Beneath Your Bed: The Surprising Story of Dust by April Pulley Sayer (2005):
Dust is made everywhere, every day.
A flower drops pollen.
A dog shakes dirt from its fur.
A butterfly flutters,
and scales fall off its wings.

It's a Butterfly's Life by Irene Kelly (2007):
A butterfly has four wings. Each wing has shimmering scales that overlap like shingles on a roof.

Take a moment to discuss the unique details presented on this page. Tell students that readers love to be shown details they might have missed or never before had the opportunity to learn. Ask, "What have you noticed that others may not have observed?" Prepare to be astounded as students tell you the number of black tiles in the hall, the spider that's made a web below the water fountain, or the way in which their music teacher clears her throat when the room gets noisy. Encourage them to continue observing the world and to include these details in their writing.

Extension: Provide students with palm-size notebooks and encourage them to record unique observations that they can include in their writing. When students do transfer a detail from their notebook to their writing, invite them to coteach the next day's mini-lesson by modeling the collecting and incorporating of information.

Staying on Track

On Hand: One or more copies of writing in which the writer has added irrelevant details. For example:

Yesterday my friend came over to play. We played with matchbox cars on the sidewalk. My friend had the sport cars and the convertibles, but I didn't mind because I had the camper and it is my favorite car of all. I like it *because it has the most doors that open and a tent that pops up. I had my new sneakers on, even though they are too big for me still.*

Mini-Lesson: Remind students that revision doesn't always mean adding details; sometimes we have to remove details that cause our writing to veer off track. Invite your class (or small groups of students, if you prefer) to stand and form a train by placing their hands on the shoulders of the student in front of them. Tell students that they will listen to a piece of writing as they move forward as a train. When the writing goes off track, they, the train, should halt.

When students regroup on the rug, ask them what a writer should do if he or she has added unnecessary details. Help them understand that all writers need to cross off the bits that don't belong.

Extension: Project your own writing in which you have crossed out words, sentences, or even whole paragraphs. Talk to students about the decisions you made.

Beware the Adjective

On Hand: Chart paper or whiteboard and a marker.

Mini-Lesson: "What do you do when students begin to overload their writing with details?" teachers often ask. The previous lesson, Staying on Track, addresses this problem, but I often find that what primary teachers are referring to when they say "too much description" is an overabundance of adjectives.

Adjectives are not necessarily details. At times the right adjective can provide the perfect picture: *yellow rubber boots*, for example, but words like *pretty, good, excellent*, and *awesome* create absolutely no picture at all. I've witnessed many a teacher conduct a word choice lesson that encourages students to retire words like good only to see sentences like this follow:

My soccer team is really, really, really awesome!!!!

Model the elimination of vague adjectives (and adverbs) where you can. Project an initial attempt:

My sweet grandmother bakes the most awesome cookies!

Remind students of "show, don't tell" and rewrite:

"Oh, I'm so glad you're here!" my grandmother says as I walk through her back door. "Sit down here and I'll pour you some tea." I have no sooner sat down when she puts a plate of chocolate peanut butter cookies down in front of me. I can tell that the centers are gooey and the edges are crisp—just the way I like them.

Discuss the difference between the first sentence and the following paragraph. Point out that awesome doesn't make our taste buds water, whereas words like *gooey* just might.

Extension: Post a list titled "Beware of These Adjectives" and record those that are too general.

March

Focus: How Do I Organize a Story? and How Do I End My Piece?

In October you and your class explored the concept of using an organizational structure, that is, the understanding that all writing has a structure—bones if you will—that helps the reader follow along (and helps the writer know in what direction to go next). This month students revisit organization, this time taking a closer look at sequencing and the pattern of story.

There are many patterns of story and they come from varied cultural traditions. One of the most common patterns (often the pattern of folk and fairy tales) is the pattern of three. I teach students this pattern while being careful to acknowledge it is one pattern and not by any means the *only* pattern. I teach it because it helps students recognize the rhythm and pacing of story. It gives their stories a direction, suspense, and a satisfying ending. It helps students move away from the typical "and then, and then, and then . . ." style of storytelling (which often ends abruptly when the writer has become bored with the topic) or the classic "bed to bed" story, in which writers share information about their characters' days from the time the characters wake up to the time they go to sleep at night. I don't present the pattern of three in one mini-lesson, but divide it into a series of lessons that not only help students write with increased attention to organization but also improve their reading comprehension. The next five lessons build an understanding of the pattern of three (and the ones that follow will assist students in writing successful endings).

Students in the primary grades should not all be expected to apply these lessons in the same way. For most kindergarten students, you are exposing them to ideas that will build their understanding of literature and story, but may not be directly applied to their own storytelling (in the same way that we practice compare and contrast or cause and effect before students are reading text that requires these necessary comprehension skills). Most first graders will eagerly apply the lesson concepts to class interactive writing but may or may not be able to bring the pattern to their own writing. The majority of second graders will begin to use these concepts in their narratives with astonishing success.

(For an introduction to organization for primary students, see "Focus: How Will I Organize My Writing?" on page 73).

Introduce the Storyboard

On Hand: Blank white paper that can be folded in quarters or storyboard graphic organizers (Figure 5.7)—one for each student.

Mini-Lesson: If you teach kindergarten, you may be wondering how to help your students transition into writing longer narratives. Draw or project a storyboard. Model the telling of a story in frames. Keep your story fairly simple, recording each event with illustration, words, or both in sequence. Modeling a story in this way tends to be enormously motivational. Suddenly your kindergarten students are writing stories with multiple events. (Note: Avoid modeling the superhero story. Kindergartners gravitate toward retelling cartoons, which result in a good deal of pseudoviolence.)

First- and second-grade students benefit from prewriting with storyboards. Model their use as a story planner. Sketch your story in the boxes. Then use the first frame to guide the writing of the first para-

Figure 5.7
Storyboard from
*The Big Book of
Reproducible
Graphic Organizers*
(Scholastic, 1999)

graph of your story. Let students know that the storyboard is *not* the full telling of the tale; it is a tool to help them think their stories through from beginning to end. Recommend that they conference with you while in the storyboard stage. Discussion often helps students bring more structure and depth to their stories.

Because of the developmental stage of primary students, or because students are familiar with graphic stories similar to those in comic books, several students will view the planner *as* the story. In other words, they will not be inclined to retell it with greater detail on paper. That's okay. There is value in sequencing a story, and what they learn through this exercise will be applied as they continue to explore story structure.

Extension: Suggest students retell their reading selections using a storyboard.

In the Beginning

On Hand: A handful of books you have read aloud in the past year in which the main character is easily identified.

Mini-Lesson: The beginning of most stories (whether they follow the pattern of three or not), introduces a character who wants something. Encourage students to think of stories they have read or heard and ask, "Who is the main character? What does the main character want?" Students adore answering these questions. The experience is akin, I believe, to getting the questions right on Jeopardy. Once they get going, they don't want to stop. Here are some possible answers:

> *Chrysanthemum* by Kevin Henkes (1991): Chrysanthemum wants a new name.
> *Knuffle Bunny: A Cautionary Tale* by Mo Willems (2004): Trixie wants Knuffle Bunny.
> *Little Pea* by Amy Kraus Rosenthal (2005): Little Pea wants to avoid candy.
> *Are You My Mother?* by P.D. Eastman (1960): Little Bird wants its mother

Story is about yearning. We keep turning the pages because we become invested in the character's desire and want him or her to succeed. By simply knowing what their characters' want at the beginning of a story, students will write with more purpose and their stories will take on more shape.

You might post a list of some of the things literary characters strive for. Suggest that your students begin a story with a character who wants something.

Extension: Suggest students look through your classroom library in search of book pairs: two characters who want similar things. Here are some possible pairings:

- Olivia and Fancy Nancy want glamour.
- Brave Charlotte and Adventure Annie want adventure.
- McDuff and Hermit Crab want a home.

Pattern of Three

On Hand: *Moon Sandwich Mom* by Jennifer Richard Jacobson (1999) or any other picture book that follows the pattern of three (see sidebar).

Mini-Lesson: Your students have come to recognize that a story often begins with a character who wants something. Does this mean the character gets

Titles Organized by the Pattern of Three

Bootsie Barker Bites by Barbara Bottner (1992).
Gator by Randy Cecil (2007).
Mrs. Toggle's Beautiful Blue Shoe by Robin Pulver (1994).
Wemberly Worried by Kevin Henkes (2000).
The Wild Woods by Simon James (1993).
Virginnie's Hat by Dori Chaconas (2007).

what he or she wants right off the bat? No way! (Not unless the character, like King Midas, is meant to learn to be careful of what one wishes.) No, typically the character:

1. Tries to get what he wants and fails. (That's right: failure is an important part of story.)
2. Again tries to get what he wants. And you know what? Again he fails.
3. Musters all his resolve and often succeeds on the third try (or after the third failure) to get what he wants—or he changes his mind. Either of these endings can work.

Ask students to look for this pattern as you read the story aloud.

Extension: Ask students to think of all the stories that have three in the title (*The Three Little Pigs, Goldilocks and the Three Bears, The Three Billy Goats Gruff, Three Wishes*) and help them to see that they also follow a three-act structure.

Writing a Story Together

On Hand: Chart paper and a marker.

Mini-Lesson: For second graders, you could do this mini-lesson for one or two days, modeling story development. For kindergarten and first grade, I suggest allowing this mini-lesson to carry over a full week. In doing so, you will have composed a class story that can be published or performed.

Each day, write one section of an interactive story that follows the pattern of three. Begin by coming up with a character and determining what the character wants. On the first day, write a paragraph that *shows* what your character wants. Point out that writers don't merely tell readers what a character wants they let us share in the wanting.

For example, don't write:

Mandy wanted a dog.

Instead, write:

> While walking home from school, Mandy heard footsteps behind her. She turned to see who was following. It was the dirtiest, mangiest dog she'd ever seen. The dog had black matted fur, and one torn ear, but it was wagging its tail as if to say, "I'm so glad I found you!"

The next day, determine what the character is going to try and how she is going to fail. Be careful not to list: "Mandy asked her mother if she could have a dog, but she said no." Instead, *show* the scene. When Mandy's mother says that Mandy is not responsible enough to have a dog, our character knows what she needs to try or prove next.

Invite students to write their own stories with the pattern of three as you continue to model. By the fifth day, your character will either succeed in getting what she wants or she will change her mind.

Extension: Suggest students search your collection for books that demonstrate the pattern of three. You might designate one book bin for these titles.

Cutting Up the Bones

On Hand: An underdeveloped story (see below), scissors, tape, and five sheets of paper.

Mini-Lesson: Even though you have spent months discussing the need for quality details, even though you have spent a week modeling the development of story, even though you have read aloud fabulous literature, you will still have students that list:

> Mandy wanted a dog, but she didn't have the money. First she tried a lemonade stand, but that didn't work. Then she tried doing chores, but that didn't work. Then she decided to work at the pet store. She made lots of money and got to buy a dog.

Use the text above to model this great revision technique. Point out to students that this piece is organized, but it lacks details. It definitely does not create a movie in the mind of the reader.

Tell students that you are going to do "surgery" to separate the bones of the story. By separating the bones you will make room to add the body. Cut the five sentences apart and tape each one to the top of a clean sheet of paper. Using the beginning of the story, demonstrate how you would expand:

> Mandy wanted a dog, but she didn't have money. Mandy knew that dogs were expensive because she visited the pet store every day. There, she had fallen in love with a little Scottish terrier puppy. The puppy jumped up and down in its cage as soon as Mandy arrived. "I have to figure out a way to make money," said Mandy. "I have to!"

Extension: Later, during writing conferences, suggest that students who have listed conduct surgery. Invite students to share their successful revisions the following day.

Reflective Endings

On Hand: Several books that have endings that mirror the beginning, such as *Wilfrid Gordon McDonald Partridge* by Mem Fox (1985), *Tacky the Penguin* by Helen Lester (1998), and *Miss Bridie Chose a Shovel* by Leslie Connor (2004). (See the sidebar for other suggestions.)

Mini-Lesson: We know that when a story follows a pattern of three, the character either gets what he wants in the end or changes his mind. But these endings—like all endings, no matter what the organizational pattern or genre—have an additional job. There has to be a beat at the end of the piece, a moment that allows the reader to respond with an "Ah," an "Ah" that means I am so glad I read this work. Reflective endings (also known as circular, loop, or wraparound endings) are one technique that helps to create this feel-good moment.

Tell students that you are going to read the beginning and ending of each book and you would like them to see if they can detect a pattern:

Titles with Reflective Endings:

Do Kangaroos Wear Seatbelts? by Jane Kurtz (2005).
Diary of a Worm by Doreen Cronin (2003).
Rotten Ralph by Jack Gantos (1976).
My Mama Had a Dancing Heart by Libba Moore (1995).
The Paper Boy by Dav Pilkey (1996).
The Relatives Came by Cynthia Rylant (1985).

Wilfrid Gordon McDonald Partridge

Beginning: *"There was once a small boy named Wilfrid Gordon McDonald Partridge and what's more he wasn't very old either."*
Ending: *"And the two of them smiled and smiled because Miss Nancy's memory had been found again by a small boy, who wasn't very old either."*

Tacky the Penguin

Beginning: *"There once lived a penguin. His home was a nice icy land he shared with his companions. His companions were named Goodly, Lovely, Angel, Neatly, and Perfect. His name was Tacky. Tacky was an odd bird."*

Figure 5.8
Primary Writing
with a Reflective
Ending

Ending: *"Goodly, Lovely, Angel, Neatly, and Perfect hugged Tacky. Tacky was an odd bird but a very nice bird to have around."*

Fishy and his mom

Fishy seid to his mom, lets play hide and seack no Fishy said Fishys mom so Fishy ran away. late that nite he was lonly. he went back to his house and got his teddy bair. he he opind the dor. Fishy, calld Fihsys mom, whare are you he ran out of the house with his teddy bair he jumt in the boshis Fishys mom wachet out side she saw the boshis mov she wacet over to the bushis I am sorry seid Fishy. we are sort of playing hide and seack seid Fishys Mom, thay lafet.

Miss Bridie Chose a Shovel

Beginning: *"She could have picked a chiming clock or a porcelain figurine, but Miss Bridie chose a shovel back in 1856."*
Ending: *"She could have had a chiming clock or a porcelain figurine, but Miss Bridie chose a shovel back in 1856."*

Students will notice, of course, that the endings use words or exact phrases from the beginnings. The reason these reflective endings are so effective is that the reader is invited on a journey and then delivered home again.

Invite students to try out reflective endings in their own work.

Extension: Draw two bookends on the board. (I often find that students are unfamiliar with bookends. Review their purpose if necessary.) Write a beginning above the first bookend, such as: "George Washington was our first president." Write a reflective ending above the second bookend: "Everyone agreed. Only George Washington could be our first president." Erase your model. Write another beginning above the first bookend. Challenge students to come up with a reflective ending.

After trying this a few times (and perhaps going in the reverse direction) invite kids to come up with both beginnings and reflective endings. See Figure 5.8 for a student sample.

Book Bag Endings

On Hand: Approximately twenty books from your classroom library that you and the students have already read, sticky notes, five or six cloth book bags, duct tape, and a permanent marker.

Mini-Lesson: In October you focused on beginnings; now it's time to do the same exercise with endings. Remind students that they have examined books with reflective endings and encourage them to look for other techniques authors use—techniques that might help them with their own endings. Read some of the endings from the books you gathered and look for similarities. It's essential that you explore books that have been previously read, or neither the power of the ending nor the technique used will be fully recognized. Allow students to come up with their own names for the technique. They might include techniques like the following:

- "Repetition," in which language, not just the beginning, is repeated (*Library Lion* by Michelle Knudson [2006] and *Chicken Joy on Redbean Road* by Jacqueline Briggs Martin [2007])
- "Joke Endings," in which the last page provides a giggle (*The House Takes a Vacation* by Jacqueline Davies [2007], *Dream Hop* by Julia Durango [2005], *Ping Pong Pig* by Caroline Jayne Church [2008])
- "Happy Endings," in which we trust that life will be fine (*Granite Baby* by Lynne Bertrand [2005] and *Those Shoes* by Maribeth Bolts [2007])
- "Surprise Endings" (*Terrific* by Jon Agee [2005] and *King Bidgood's in the Bathtub* by Audrey Wood [1993])

Once you've determined categories (sticky notes can help you keep track), use a strip of duct tape and a permanent marker to label the bags with the categories. Encourage students to add to the bags when they find books that fit.

Extension: Suggest that students examine their own work and list the types of endings they've used.

April

Focus: How Do I Write Poetry?

April is National Poetry Month and the perfect time to revisit voice. It is through poetry that many a writer (particularly struggling writers) experience the power of their own words. Those who sometimes feel daunted by the complexity of thought (How can I tell everything that happened?) and the vastness of the page (How long does it have to be?) experience enormous freedom when encouraged to select evocative words and place them in stanzas. Through poetry, our students are able to convey big thoughts; we get a glimpse of the deep emotional terrain they navigate even when they are not yet able to fully articulate their deep thinking.

Primary students often equate poetry with rhyming, and although many poems do rhyme, I do not recommend you focus on this particular style. Why? Creating meaningful rhyming poetry requires both a broad vocabulary and dexterity with words. Typically, when young children focus on word endings, they sacrifice both fluency and poignancy. We get a sort of meaningless word play:

> I saw a dog.
> Sitting on a log.
> With a hog.

And although this does create a fun image, the words bounce right off us. Opportunities for connection are lost.

Instead, be explorers of poetry. Don your binoculars and take a close look at author's craft. How do authors arrange words in free verse? What do they do with line breaks, white space, and font? What types of words do they choose? How do poems tickle our senses, our thoughts, our emotions?

Begin, of course, by reading lots and lots of poetry. Okay, go ahead and read some Shel Silverstein and Jack Prelutsky,

Recommended Poetry

Butterfly Eyes and Other Secrets of the Meadow by Joyce Sidman (2006).

A Curious Collection of Cats by Betsy Franco (2009).

Doodle Dandies: Poems That Take Shape by J. Patrick Lewis (2002).

Here's a Little Poem: A Very First Book of Poetry edited by Jane Yolen and Andrew Fusek Peters (2007).

Hip Hop Speaks to Children, edited by Nikki Giovanni (2008).

Inside Out: Children's Poets Discuss Their Work by JonArno Lawson (2008).

A Kick in the Head: An Everyday Guide to Poetic Forms by Paul B. Janeczko (2005).

A River of Words: The Story of William Carlos Williams by Jen Bryant (2008).

Speak to Me (And I Will Listen Between the Lines) by Karen English (2004).

There Is a Flower at the Tip of My Nose Smelling Me by Alice Walker (2006).

Thunderboom! Poems for Everyone by Charlotte Pomerantz (2006).

but again—be careful not to focus too heavily on this one type of humorous, rhyming deliciousness. (You might save these books for the end of the month). Check out the books recommended in the sidebar for some fabulous models.

Once you begin your exploration of poetry, I bet you'll conclude that a month isn't nearly enough.

A Poem Is a Photograph

On Hand: *Speak to Me (And I Will Listen Between the Lines)* by Karen English (2004) or other poetry that speaks to the lives of your students, and photographs of familiar sights for students: backpack, cafeteria, school bus, playground, desk, sidewalk, and so on.

Mini-Lesson: Read *Speak to Me* (or your selected poetry book) and then reread it from beginning to end. (*Speak to Me* is about six urban kids and it begs to be read over and over again.) Take a moment to ask students what they observed about the poetry. They may make connections: "I have a pen with pink ink like Rica," or "I felt like Brianna when Siobhan didn't want to be my friend anymore." Or they may begin to notice that a poem can be long like "Walking Home Makes Me Feel Good" or incredibly short like "Five More Minutes and I Get to Go Home":

> Five more minutes and I'll get to go home
> What else is there to say?

Tell students that whereas a story or a personal narrative has a beginning, middle, and end—a poem can be compared to a photograph in which a single moment (and all of its meaning and ensuing emotion) is captured in time. Show them the photographs you have collected and choose one to model the first draft of a poem:

> Brand new composition notebook
> Smelling like fresh air
> A place for my name
> White pages, blue lines
> Not yet marred by
> Wobbly letters,
> Misspelled words,

Crossed off thoughts.
My words
Not yet placed on the pages
Still sparkle in the breeze

Make any changes that occur to you. (My last line was originally "Still glow," but I crossed it off and explained to students that I wanted to use an image that connected to my line: "Smelling like fresh air.") You might spend time later revising your poem. If so, share your revisions during author's chair or another mini-lesson.

Invite students to use the photographs you've collected to write their own poems.

Extension: Suggest students bring in their own photographs from home to inspire their poetry.

Observing Poets Observing

On Hand: *Song of the Water Boatman & Other Pond Poems* by Joyce Sidman (2005).

Mini-Lesson: This award-winning picture book presents a poem and a scientific paragraph for each of the pond subjects. Consider the following full-page spread on peepers. On the left-hand side we read a poem that begins with this stanza:

Listen for me on a spring night
On a wet night
On a rainy night,
Listen for me on a still night,
For in the night I sing

And on the right-hand page we read these first two sentences of a paragraph:

The sound of spring peepers is one of the earliest signs of spring. These inch-long tree frogs can freeze almost completely in winter because of special "antifreeze" in their cells.

This text is best digested slowly, so you might want to conduct this mini-lesson over several days.

Write a chart of observations about the poems. The chart might look something like the one in Figure 5.9.

Figure 5.9
Poem Observation Chart

Observation	Example
Some poems repeat words.	"Peck, peck/Crackle, crackle/Fluff, fluff"
Sometimes the words create a picture.	"L e a p I n g"
Poets use stanzas and break up sentences. Sometimes the lines begin with a capital letter and sometimes they don't.	"Here kicks the frog with golden eyes that gulps the bug that nabs the nymph"
Some first lines of poems begin with the same word.	"Here hang" "Here floats" "Here nods"
There is lots of space around some of the poems.	"Smart young caddis worms select only"
Some poems rhyme and some do not, and some poems do both.	"Song of the Water Boatman" does both.

Extension: Invite students to choose a subject they know a great deal about and write a poem pertaining to that subject. If you made a list titled "Things We Know About," as suggested on page 52, you might want to take a moment to review it and add any new interests that come to mind.

Most Amazing Thing

On Hand: Whiteboard

Mini-Lesson: On your whiteboard write the prompt: "The most amazing thing I ever saw was . . ." Invite students who do not have a topic to give this one a try. This is a particularly powerful prompt producing unforgettable opening lines: "The most amazing thing I ever saw was my father eat a ladybug . . ."

Extension: Compile the poetry in a class book.

Where I'm From

On Hand: The poem "Where I'm From" By George Ella Lyon (you can find it online).

Mini-Lesson: In this poem, George Ella Lyon shares specific details from her past that have helped to define her. Read the poem to students. Here are a couple of my favorite lines from the second stanza:

> I'm from fudge and eyeglasses,
>   from Imogene and Alafair.
> I'm from the know-it-alls
>   and the pass-it-ons,
> from Perk up! and Pipe down!

Model writing your own "I am from" poem, perhaps beginning with the concrete and including what others have said to you:

> I am from birch trees and chickadees
> from dry your hair with the canister vacuum hose—reversed
> I am from the Not now's, Not here's, You will never be's
> And do you expect to be happy all the time? (yes)

Invite students to write their own "I am from" poem. Suggest they draw first—the prewriting will help them pick out concrete details and "hear" the voices that are a part of their everyday lives.

Extension: Introduce other poems as scaffolding. You might use Paul Janeczko's book *A Kick in the Head: An Everyday Guide to Poetic Forms* (2005), which demonstrates twenty-nine forms, or simply choose a favorite poem and challenge students to write one using the same pattern.

Found Poetry

On Hand: An article (perhaps from your weekly student newspaper) or a nonfiction passage you have read for science or social studies prepared to project, a whiteboard, chart paper, markers, and index cards (a small stack for pairs of students).

Mini-Lesson: Project a passage of text, such as this one from *Owen and Mzee: The True Story of a Remarkable Friendship* by Isabella Hatkoff, Craig Hatkoff, and Dr. Paula Kahumba (2006).

> *As the weeks went on, Owen and Mzee spent more and more time together. Soon, they were inseparable. Their bond remains strong to this day. They swim together, eat together, drink together, and sleep next to each other. They rub noses.*

Ask students to pick out words or phrases they find particularly powerful. Together, arrange these words into a poem. Feel free to add words to enhance meaning. Here is an example:

Owen and Mzee
Together
Inseparable bond
Swim together
Eat
Drink
And sleep
Together
They rub noses
Owen and Mzee

Play with the line breaks and word order. Let students know that there are many possibilities. Invite them to work in pairs and choose their own texts. Have them record words that particularly speak to them on cards, and then use the cards to arrange the language into a poem. (Remind students that they might want to leave some of the cards out.) Encourage those happy with their poems to copy them down on paper. Figure 5.10a and 5.10b show a student's poem before and after revision.

Extension: Suggest students find words that appeal to them in magazines, cut them out, and then, perhaps adding to those words, arrange them in a poem.

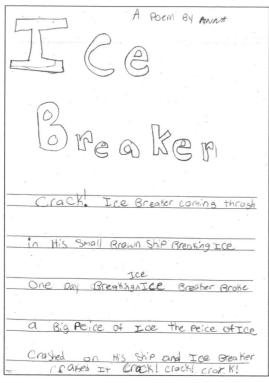

Figure 5.10a
In her first version, Anna records her ideas in a familiar prose pattern. She includes onomatopoeia, but shifts to narrative style with "One day."

Figure 5.10b
Anna uses line breaks in her revisions, and although the "One day" remains, the work takes shape as a dramatic poem.

Internal Rhyme

<u>On Hand:</u>   *River Friendly River Wild* by Jane Kurtz (2000) and/or *Banjo Granny* by Sarah Martin Busse and Jacqueline Briggs Martin (2006), or any other poems with internal rhyme.

<u>Mini-Lesson:</u> Young children who have already come to equate poetry with rhyming words may loathe giving up end rhymes. Encourage these students to use internal rhymes, as Jane Kurtz does when describing sandbagging during a Red River flood:

>   Wrist twist 'till the bag's closed

or as Busse and Martin do in their lyrical picture book:

He was a baby who went wiggly, jiggly, and all–around giggly, and tip over tumble for bluegrass music . . .

Point out the playfulness of internal rhyme and how lovely it sounds to the ear. Suggest students try including internal rhyme in their poetry.

Extension: The poetry in *River Friendly River Wild* came from Jane Kurtz's own experience of losing her home in the flooding of the Red River Valley (on her birthday no less). As she coped with the tasks at hand, she stopped to record the details that are included in these poems. Invite students to think of an experience they've had and suggest they brainstorm a list details and then compose a poem from their memory list.

Word Play

On Hand: Whiteboard, marker, and a copy of the poem "Jabberwocky" by Lewis Carroll.

Mini-Lesson: This classic poem can be found online, in poetry anthologies, in picture books, and where it was originally published in its entirety: *Through the Looking Glass.* It's interesting to note that Lewis Carroll (real name Charles Dodgson) wrote the first verse when he was a child—subsequent verses were developed when he was playing a game with his cousins. Note that in this poem the Jabberwock is slain and the boy comes galumphing back with its head. You may want to say that you're making an exception to your "no violence" rule (if you have one) so students might see what this amazing poet could do with word-play. If you are simply too uncomfortable, you might share just the first two verses:

> **The Jaberwocky by Lewis Carroll**
> `Twas brillig, and the slithy toves
> Did gyre and gimble in the wabe;
> All mimsy were the borogoves,
> And the mome raths outgrabe.
> `Beware the Jabberwock, my son!
> The jaws that bite, the claws that catch!
> Beware the Jubjub bird, and shun
> The frumious Bandersnatch!'

Read the poem aloud with much expression. Point out to students that poets often use rhyme in poetry, but there are many other ways to play with words as well. Carroll created many of the nonsense words in Jabberwocky by combining words. Two of the words galumphing (*gallop* and *triumphant*) and chortled (*chuckled* and *snort*) have made it into the English dictionary. Choose a word such as *slithy* and have students guess which words Lewis combined. (He combined *slimy* and *lithe*, but students might also suggest *slippery, slithery,* and others.)

Now write an action sentence on the board ("The bear walked down the path," for example) and, with students, play with the words:

The Grizlout grambled down the troad.

You get the idea. Tell students that inventing words is a favorite activity of many poets as well as writers of other genres.

Extension: Reread the poem while students are sitting at their desks. Encourage them to draw an illustration of the Jabberwock. They may also wish to include the Jubjub bird and the Bandersnatch in their pictures. Afterward ask, "What words from the poem helped shape your creatures?"

Repeating Letter Sounds

On Hand: Poem containing alliteration and/or consonance, such as Dennis Lee's "Silvery": "Silverly/ Silverly,/ Over the/ Trees/ The moon drifts/ By on a/ Runaway/ Breeze."

Mini-Lesson: Project the poem or write it on chart paper so students can examine it.

Tell students that writers often choose to use lots of the same letter sounds in their poetry to create a certain effect. (Alliteration is repetition of the same beginning consonant sounds: Peter Piper picked a peck of pickled peppers. Consonance is the repetition of consonant sounds elsewhere in words—frequently at the end of words. Assonance is the repetition of vowel sounds.)

Dennis Lee's poem is a lullaby so it's not surprising that he used a good deal of words that either begin or end with the *s* sound—similar to the *shhh* sound a mother makes to quiet her child. Ask students to count the number of times they hear the *s* sound. Point out that it's not the actual letter they are looking for, but the sound. The word *breeze* provides an *s* sound.

Invite students to try this technique in their poetry.

Extension: Share the poem "In Bed With Cuddly Creatures" by Wes Magee: "Who's tucked up with me in bed?/ Peter Panda/ and Foxy Fred." The poem goes on to name all the animals whose names are alliterative. Both this poem and the Lee poem mentioned above can be found in a fabulous anthology: *Here's a Little Poem: A Very First Book of Poetry* edited by Jane Yolen and Andrew Fusek Peters (2007).

May

Focus: How Do I Choose the Strongest, Most Effective Words?

Focusing on strong word choice is a wonderful way to wind down the year. Attention to word choice will help students integrate what they've learned during the school year and will strengthen several of the other traits as well: ideas, voice, and fluency.

In December you inspired a love of words, introduced onomatopoeia, and identified lively verbs. This month students will be given the opportunity to reinforce that knowledge and will also look at precise nouns, shades of meaning in adjectives, and specific vocabularies.

Words, Words, Words

On Hand: Whiteboard, marker, and copies of brainstorming graphic organizer.

Mini-Lesson: Share with students the prewriting strategy of brainstorming words that *might* appear in new work. This will help them to tap into their specific vocabularies and spend extra time thinking about strong verbs and sensory words.

Choose one of your areas of interest. For example, I would choose tennis, pool, knitting, cooking, rock climbing, or dogs. Introduce your topic and write a key word at the top of the board. For example, I might say, "I want to write about my struggle with learning to knit," and write the word, *knitting.*

Now draw a three-column chart:

Knitting		
Things	**Actions**	**Place (create a movie)**
Needles	Knit	Cozy living room
Yarn	Purl	Couch
Directions	Cast on	Smell of wool
Loops	Drop a stitch	Chatter from friends
Fingers	Wrap	
Knots	Count	
Holes	Tear out	
	Help	
	Practice	
	Untangle	

Bounce from column to column, filling in the words that come to you. Model how the recollection of one word helps you think of an action. For example, the word *knot*, makes me think of *untangle*. Share your observations of the process: "When I record my words, I not only think of better words—words that create a picture—but I also begin to plan my piece." (You may want to cross words off your list right then and there. I substituted *chatter* for *talking*, for instance.) Remind students that you may not need all of the words and that you'll continue to choose the words that work best.

Offer a copy of the brainstorming graphic organizer for those students who would like to prewrite by brainstorming words. Place extra copies in the writing center. (Note: one benefit from this prewriting exercise is that primary students really stay with a piece, developing their ideas as they weave in the words.)

Extension: After reading a picture book, ask students to complete the same three-column chart, this time recalling the memorable words the author used.

Pirate Talk

On Hand: *How I Became a Pirate* by Melinda Long (2003)

Mini-Lesson: Tell students that many subjects have a special vocabulary. List several words and see if your students can identify the topic:

- scales, gills, fins
- hoop, dribble, jump shot
- neck, strings, bow

Encourage students to provide lists of words and have classmates come up with the subject. Remind students that when they use specific words like these, their writing is more captivating, more believable.

Show students the mentor text, *How I Became a Pirate*. Tell them that Melinda Long's book is made all the more enjoyable because of the use of pirate talk. Read the story, inviting students to give a thumbs-up every time they hear specific pirate language.

Extension: Other books that model the use of specific language are *Jingle the Brass* by Patricia Newman (2004) (train language) and *A Good Day's Fishing* by James Prosek (2004) (fishing terminology).

Substituting Better Words

On Hand: Whiteboard, marker, and chart paper.

Mini-Lesson: On the chart paper write the following sentence:

They went into a store that smelled and saw lots of things.

Time to Bury the "Said Is Dead" Chart

Believe it or not, most professional writers wouldn't be caught dead using all those synonyms for *said*. "The word *said* is invisible," an editor told me after reading a manuscript of my first picture book, "Use *said* whenever possible." It is commonly accepted that the overuse of *replied, commented, exclaimed,* and *shouted* is a sign of an amateur. (Sometimes writers use synonyms that are terribly unlikely. Try giggling a sentence, for example.) Students will pick up the occasional synonym from their reading (great!) and will from time to time wish to indicate a whisper or a shout, but try not to encourage the scattering of *said* synonyms.

Ask students to discuss the quality of the words chosen in this sentence. Help them to understand that the language is too vague. Ask questions like these: How did they go into the store? What kind of store? What did the store smell like? What were the things they saw?

On the board, make a four-box graphic organizer (see Figure 5.11). With students, brainstorm a list of more precise verbs and more specific nouns. Let them know that it's often best to name schools, streets, stores, and so on, even if they wish to make up a name. Naming gives a piece more voice and a sense of validity. Students, in their eagerness, will often offer a type of

Figure 5.11
Specific Word
Choice

Went		Store	
Raced		Home Depot	
Sprinted		Stop and Save	
Trudged		Martha's Fudge Shop	
Marched		Handy Andy's	
Snuck		Get and Go	
Sauntered		Second Time Around	
Skipped			
Flew			
Wandered			
Smelled of		Things	
Vanilla		Ponchos with fringe	
Bacon		Hammers	
Sawdust		Orange marshmallow peanuts	
Chocolate		Dusty pickle jars	
Moth balls		Ripe cherries	

store: candy store. Show them that the name "Martha's Fudge Shop" is far more fun and evocative. When students suggest clothing for things, invite them to be even more specific: ponchos with fringe, red cowboy boots, pants covered in pockets.

Once you have filled your graphic, have students work in pairs to create enticing sentences:

> They raced into Home Depot, which smelled of sawdust, and saw a wall of hammers.
>
> They snuck in Martha's Fudge Shop, which smelled of chocolate, and saw rows of orange marshmallow peanuts.

After you have revised sentences, you can also tweak the remaining verbs for *smell* (*reeked, stunk, wafted*) and *saw* (*spotted, noticed, glimpsed, glazed, glanced, observed, stared*).

Extension: Read Chapter 5 of *Harry Potter and the Sorcerer's Stone* by J.K. Rowling (1998)—in particular, the description of the apothecary in Diagon Alley:

[Hagrid and Harry] visited the Apothecary, which was fascinating enough to make up for its horrible smell, a mixture of bad eggs and rotted cabbages. Barrels of slimy stuff stood on the floor; jars of herbs, dried roots, and bright powders lined the walls; bundles of feathers, strings of fangs, and snarled claws hung from the ceiling.

Tightening Sentences

On Hand: Whiteboard and a marker.

Mini-Lesson: Occasionally, post sentences on your whiteboard and ask students to both tighten and liven them by using more specific language. Here are some examples:

> The animal doctor walked slowly away from the hospital.
> (The vet trudged away from Cumberland Animal Clinic.)

> Big dogs had fun in the city square.
> (Great Danes frolicked in Central Park.)

Ask students to take a closer look at their writing to see if there are places where they could tighten or substitute vivid words.

Extension: Ask students to hunt for sentences that they admire in picture books. Then invite the class to "melt the sentences down." In other words, ask them to take lively language and turn it into the banal, as students did with this sentence from *Nothing Happens on 90th Street* by Roni Schotter (1999):

> *Mr. Chang was arranging fish fillets in his newly opened Seafood Emporium.*

Rewrite:

A man was working in a new fish shop.

Shades of Meaning

On Hand: Whiteboard and a marker.

Mini-Lesson: Brainstorming a list of substitutes for vague, generic words (such as *walk* and *nice*) can be difficult for students at any age, but especially for primary students. What you might notice is that once a student has offered the first substitute, others of the same connotation are suggested. For example, if you ask for synonyms for *walked* and the first child offers *runs*, students follow with *raced, sprinted,* and *flew*. So instead of simply listing synonyms, draw a line across your board. As you place the synonyms on the string, student will quickly come to recognize that words with opposite values are at each end. Here is what this looks like:

←———→

trudge   plod   amble   saunter   stroll   jog   trot   run   race   gallop   dash   sprint   fly

←———→

freezing   icy   frosty   cold   chilly   cool   warm   steamy   hot   boiling   sweltering   sizzling

Just by offering the range, students will provide many more words, and you'll find yourself discussing shades of meaning. Although the activity is open-ended, the discussion that ensues is fabulous for the acquisition of new words.

Extension: Have students write as many sentences as they can about a topic such as recess, but here's the catch: They may only use each word once. That includes *and, the, in, on,* and so on. This brief exercise helps students think carefully about word choice and gives them practice in coming up with synonyms. Although I don't often suggest using a prompt, in this case it's fun for students to see how classmates approached the task.

Riddles

On Hand: Whiteboard or chart paper, marker, and a few "What am I?" riddles, such as:

> Drip, drop,
> plop,
> plop,
> plop.
> I shower from clouds.
> What am I?
> *(rain)*

These can be found online, in riddle books, or you can write your own.

<u>Mini-Lesson:</u>   Share with students several "What am I?" or "Who am I?" riddles. Point out that riddles have *word referents*, which are words that refer to something without naming it.

Model the brainstorming of word referents. Choose an answer for a riddle, such as cat, and write a list of possible referents. (Although students may offer suggestions, write your own ideas so no one will be offended as you select two or three referents to become part of your riddle.)

> Whiskered
> Four paws
> Pointed ears
> Long tail
> Purring pet
> Meowing mammal
> Mouse pouncing
> Kibble eating
> Fur ball

Then, using these referents, write your own riddle. Demonstrate the need to choose only your *best* ideas. Think out loud as you write your riddle: "I won't use four paws, because so many animals have four paws. And I think I won't use *meowing mammal*. Even though I like the alliteration—those two *m*'s together—*meowing* makes my riddle too easy. I do like *purring* though, and may use it near the end of my riddle. Oooh, I just had an idea for making my riddle fun. I'm going to repeat the word *on*":

> Whiskers on face
> Pounces on mice
> Purrs on lap
> What am I?

Reinforce the idea of brainstorming many ideas before choosing the ones that work for your riddle. Figure 5.12 is an example of one student's riddle poem.

<u>Extension:</u>   Invite students to bring in "mystery" objects in paper bags. Allow students to take turns providing clues while classmates guess what's inside.

Figure 5.12
Abby's Riddle

Name: ABBY   6\4\09

in   the   tan   sand

sing   Brily. Silvering
gowing   in the bakr

bakr   nite

how am I   I

In the tan sand
shining brightly. Silverying
glowing in the dark, dark, night
Who am I?
(a rock)

Chapter 6

The Secret to Independence: A Desire to Write

As I hope you've begun to realize, writing independence does not occur in the primary grades because students have gained sufficient skill in writing their letters or using the frequently used word list, but because they have taken ownership of their writing. Writing has personal meaning for these young students, and they find reward not only in the act of writing but also in all the successes, big and small, that you've built into your writing program.

If you do not yet have the independence you hoped for, ask yourself the following questions:

- Do students write daily?
- Do I allow students to choose their own topics?
- Do I give students access to writing materials?
- Do I write when my students are writing?
- Do I point specifically to what they are doing well?
- Do I provide a daily opportunity for students to share their writing?
- Do I invite students to publish their work on an *individual* basis?
- Do I invite students to coteach mini-lessons with me?

To truly understand the power of these seemingly small structures, imagine the quintessential day for one student; we'll call her Stella.

On the school bus, one of the older girls offers to share her seat with Stella. She has a string and shows Stella how to play cat's cradle. Honored to be sitting with this fourth grader and thrilled to have learned the game, Stella thinks, "This is what I'm going to write about today."

During morning meeting, Mrs. Desanctis tells the students that she heard the loveliest sentence yesterday. Then she invites Stella to coteach the mini-lesson with her. Stella steps up and reads from her work the sentence that Mrs. Desanctis identifies: "My bed is like a boat that takes me places." All of her classmates agree; that is one really cool sentence.

"It's a simile," says Mrs. Desanctis. "When we say that something is *like* something else, we create a simile. Maybe, like Stella, some of you will write similes today."

During writing time, Stella hears a classmate say, "Ask Stella if that is a simile, she's an expert on those."

Stella does write about her bus ride, and during a conference, Mrs. Desanctis reflects what Stella has written: "You wrote about sitting with an older girl on the bus today and how she taught you to play cat's cradle." Stella nods, smiling. She's pleased that her teacher knows this facet of her life. "I especially like this ending," says Mrs. Desanctis: "'I hope she asks me again.' It lets us feel how special this time was." Stella and her teacher discuss how to add some information for clarification, and then Stella returns to work on her writing more. She's eager to revise, not because she wants a good grade, but because (1) it allows her to spend more time with this topic and (2) she's going to share it at author's chair and she doesn't want her classmates to ask the same questions Mrs. Desanctis asked. When adding necessary information, Stella recalls something the girl said to her and she adds the dialogue as well.

After recess, Stella shares her piece in author's chair. When she finishes, all hands shoot up for pointing. Stella smiles as her classmates point to her focus, details, and ending. Mrs. Desanctis raises her hand and points to the line of dialogue. "You added dialogue as well as clarifying information. I think we should talk about publishing this piece. Perhaps you could share it with the girl on the bus."

Certainly not all days are this rewarding for students. There will be days when students choose topics that lack energy for them, you suggest they make changes that seem *really hard*, and when all the slots for author's chair are filled.

As a professional writer, I am intimately familiar with both types of days. Sometimes the writing itself feels magical and I experience the joy of having created something wholly original. There are breakthrough days when I suddenly know how to fix a problem that's been plaguing me—when revision actually feels fun. There are days when I receive an offer of publication or a letter from a fan.

Then there are the other days—the days that are, quite frankly, more frequent. Days when the words won't come, or the ideas refuse to line up in a satisfactory manner. Days when my email holds only rejection notes from editors and gentle (but brutally honest) critiques from my writing buddies.

Nevertheless, real writers plug on. Why? Because the bright days are so very bright, and because we are members of a writing community. We know that all writers struggle from time to time, that writing can be difficult on some days, but there is always help . . . and the help, the collaboration, usually leads us back to those breakthroughs.

You can provide this community of writers. Your students can be real writers.

What if you do all of the things listed at the beginning of this chapter and still your students seem unable to write for more than five minutes independently? It may mean that in some small (yet perhaps easily fixable) way, they are being trained to be dependent. See if any of the following problems describe your situation.

I try to conduct mini-lessons, but my students talk, wiggle, fool around —basically everything except listen.

Meeting times need to acquire a warm, but serious, tone. The message is, "This is an important time when we writers come together to talk about what makes good writing."

This is a hard tone to establish if students are seated at tables or desks. The message of that arrangement is, "I'm the teacher up here conducting a lesson, so you better listen up." One of the first things you'll want to do is bring in a rug where students can congregate and *be teachers* as well as learners.

Next, make sure you spend more time reinforcing positive student participation than correcting behavioral issues. What I often see is a teacher discussing writing but addressing students directly only when telling them to sit up, stop talking, or leave the meeting area.

Initially it will be hard to focus more on reinforcing the positive behaviors you see, but try to turn your meetings around by only rewarding writing talk and ignoring other behaviors. Here are some of the ways you can punch up your positive reinforcement:

- When making observations about writing that is on the overhead or chart paper, circle a student's contribution and put his or her initials next to the circle.
- Say: "Wow, Jason, that's a really good observation. I'm going to try and do that with *my own* writing today."
- Attach particular skills to students. If Aidan pointed out the use of quotation marks, when referring to them again say, "Oh, here we need Aidan's quotation marks."
- Of course there's the ever cheesy but highly effective: "Are you sure you're a first grader, Latisha? That's a fourth-grade observation!"

Before long your students will not tolerate nonwriterly behavior.

I have conducted mini-lessons on choosing a topic, but I still have students who say they have nothing to write about.

Do you offer author's chair on a regular basis? Nothing sparks writing ideas more than listening to one's peers' work. Marissa shares her piece on sledding down a neighbor's hill. Her story reminds Nicholas of his snow fort, Tyler of the day he knocked a tooth out skating, and Petra of making snow from cotton balls in daycare. Three new ideas spawned from the sharing of one story!

Many teachers have been instructed to limit their primary students to personal narratives. I know this suggestion comes from good intentions. The thinking is that we are all better writers when we write what we know—that the best details (a very important skill for primary students) come from our own memories. However, accepting or modeling only one genre can be quite limiting. Some students simply do not recognize the gold in their everyday experiences. However, these same students can write fabulous fiction (yes, primary students can write wonderfully inventive stories) or how-to pieces. Many boys will write for hours about their passions, be it tropical fish, monster trucks, or professional wrestlers. One of my favorite pieces was directions on how to change the oil in a dirt bike.

As teachers, we can help students recognize their own topics. When a child comes rushing in to tell us that there was an unexpected visitor at their home last night, or that their father brought home take-out, or that their baby sister took her first step, say: "Oh, that would make a wonderful topic for writing time! I do hope you'll give me a chance to talk to you more about this in a writing conference."

I have one student who wants to write about the same thing day after day.

Many adult writers have made a career of writing on the same themes. As long as the student is growing as a writer—learning new skills, applying the mini-lessons, revising—I see nothing wrong with this.

With a more traditional writing class, we expect to see students produce a product a day. But there is no value to all of these products if the student is roughly producing the same work—say, five sentences —to meet the daily requirement. A child who chooses one topic and stays with that piece over time is apt to stretch his or her writing muscles.

Some of our young students will choose a new subject every day. Young children are very much in the moment, so kindergarten and early first graders are apt to write about whatever comes to mind first (or whatever emerges, sometimes quite unexpectedly, from their drawings). By the middle of first grade, however, students are beginning to sustain writing projects over days, and some over weeks. The question to ask is: "Is this student continuing to grow? Continuing to apply new skills?" If the answer is yes, then the topic is working. If not, then it's fair to ask the student to choose a new subject so he or she can continue to develop as a writer.

I have kids who write only of war, TV shows, or video games.

Ah, yes. I had this class too. Day after day a group of boys would draw pictures of guns or bombs blasting. These were not kids whose parents had gone to war, nor was it because wartime images were flashing on their TV screens at night, but they loved drawing these images in the same way they loved playing with toys that resembled guns. Their writing had become an extension of pretend play.

And yes, each year I have more and more students who want to retell the plots of movie and TV shows or re-create the action of a video game. The problem with these topics is that they're virtual —one dimensional—and it's almost impossible to help young students who choose these topics to grow as writers. The guns blast, the character moves from one level to the next—beginning, middle, and end of story.

I've also found that students who write about the things they see on screens do not have a genuine understanding of what their reading audience requires to comprehend their piece. I once tried to conference with a child who wrote about a TV show that had "twenty-six ladies who have suitcases." I tried my best to understand:

"Where are the women going?"

"Nowhere."

"Nowhere? Why do they have suitcases?"

"They're supposed to."

Of course I howled when I finally had the opportunity to watch the show: *Deal or No Deal.*

So I suggest the rule, "No writing about violence or something you've seen on a screen." You can tell students that (1) you can't help them grow as writers when they write about something virtual and (2) anything that makes others uncomfortable (violence, profanity, bathroom talk) is not an acceptable school topic choice.

My students are unable to "stretch out" words without me.

I've often observed primary teachers saying the needed word very slowly, over and over again, allowing the student to hear each separate sound. If a sound (typically a vowel sound) isn't heard, the teacher will go back and make the sound again. Before long, students feel they need the teacher in order to hear all the phonemes correctly.

Instead, have *students* say the word. Then ask, "What sounds do you hear?" When they tell you the sounds and record the letters that make those sounds, nod your head and move on. Do not try to help them to identify the phonemes they're not hearing. This is a developmental process. The more they practice (without you) the better they'll get at stretching words.

My students still want me to spell words for them.

This is a hard habit to break, but in order to do so you must be incredibly consistent. What often happens is that a teacher will announce to the class, "Please do not ask me for spellings. I want you to record the sounds you hear." Then, distracted, she'll walk by a student who asks, "How do you spell *Jersey*?" and before you know it, she's provided all six letters.

You can't. You simply can't spell *any* word. Not even if it's a difficult word, a word all your students should know, or the only word that particular student will need to create a practically perfect piece.

You can say, however:

- Record the sounds you hear
- Check your word list
- Look up at the word wall
- Circle it and we'll find the spelling later

These suggestions all help students build independence as they're writing.

What do I do with students who are developmentally young or need a great deal of writing assistance?

Herein lies the beauty of writer's workshop: It allows us to truly differentiate. Each child works at his or her own level. Some children are drawing and scribbling, while others are writing paragraphs.

Nevertheless, as teachers we are acutely aware of the varying needs and often feel pulled in many directions at once. How will Justin learn his letters if we don't sit down beside him? And how long will Nicole work before she's flitting around the room disrupting others?

I often choose to invite children to work beside me at the conference table. I don't use this as a punishment. Instead I might say to the student, "Justin, I'd love to help you with your letters today. Would you sit beside me so I can work with you more often?" Then while waiting for each new student to pull together his or her story for a conference, I lean over and help Justin identify another letter–sound combination. (If the student can remain focused and honor the needs of other writers, I might send him on a "letter interview." Having just taught him the sound of the letter *l*, I'll suggest he interview classmates for words that begin with this letter. He then draws a picture of each response on his letter page.)

I'll also extend an invitation to the child who has difficulty remaining on task. While at the conference table, she'll often stop writing to listen to the conversation, but I'd rather she listen to writing instruction than interrupt her busy classmates.

And it's essential, of course, that we find many opportunities for these students to coteach mini-lessons, participate in author's chair, and publish their work. All writers require an audience.

What do I say to students who want to write together?

I usually say, "Yes, for one go." Writers of all ages learn when they collaborate. And for students who have difficulty recording text or staying focused, a partner often makes an enormous difference. However, I do ask that students collaborate on one project only. Why? Because over time, partnerships form patterns that stilt growth: One child provides all the ideas, while the other is always the scribe.

I have students who are capable but will waste an entire writing period without getting anything down.

This is where the date stamp comes in handy. With it I can easily see what has been produced at the end of each day.

First question the student to see if there is a legitimate reason why he or she is not writing. I once had a student burst into tears. His family was in crisis, and he had been told not to tell anyone. He was afraid to write for fear of revealing the only thing that was on his mind.

Perhaps the student has trouble with transitions and therefore stops writing each and every time he or she has to begin a new piece. (Many writers are fine once they've recorded the first sentence.) If so, help the student compose the lead and see if he or she can take it from there. The student with this difficulty usually has greater success when working with one piece over a long stretch of time rather than trying to write a new product each day.

Does the student have good ideas but poor fine motor skills? These are the students I worry about most. Because writing is so laborious, they often decide early on that they "hate writing." It's not composing they hate (in fact, some of these students are my most imaginative); it's the effort of forming letter after letter. Once a student like this reaches third grade, I recommend teaching him or her computer skills. Students with fine motor difficulties often do remarkably well once they have access to a keyboard. But in the primary grades, we need a different strategy. Some possibilities: have the student write part of the period and then dictate additional sentences to you, or have the student tell his or her story into a tape recorder and then later, you type it up for him. And finally, suggest the student collaborate with another student, each one taking a turn at recording their ideas.

And yes, there are some students who simply resist. (Some very talented professional writers will admit to needing deadlines to produce—deadlines with consequences if unmet.) For these writers I point to the date stamps and simply say, "On Monday you only wrote three words and on Tuesday no words at all. I can't teach you to write well if you don't write. I think you owe me two writing periods. You'll need to stay in for recess to make those periods up." Forevermore the end of each writing period looms like a deadline.

What do I do about the child who has written very little but expands her story during author's chair?

I allow it. This student is showing what she knows—stories need detail, suspense, and voice—before she is able to execute all those words. And she's practicing fluency. She may even be willing to go back and add some of the detail she provided while sharing.

In just a short time, she will become too self-conscious to add on in this way. As she grows, so will her writing, and she will abstain from embellishing.

What do I do about the student who wants to share but can't remember what he wrote?

As I circle around in the kindergarten classroom (or sometimes first grade at the beginning of the year), I ask permission to record my words (in pencil very discreetly) at the bottom of the page so we might remember what was written on that day. Students never mind. Before author's chair they'll come to me and say, "Mrs. Jacobson, what did I write?" I read their work to them and then they proudly share.

In all first-grade classrooms there are usually one or two students, even in the end of the year, who automatically come to me to record their words for them.

My kids love to share, but a few are shy and others can't hear them. Asking them to speak up hasn't worked.

The shy child not only speaks softly but also often hides behind her work. The papers block interaction between the reader and the audience. A teacher I met on the road introduced this idea: set up a music stand. Children place their writing on the stand and project their voices as they read. They can pause to show the pictures as they go.

You can also provide students with a microphone. Speaking into a microphone provides fun in addition to courage, and all students will want a turn.

Final Words

Initiative, motivation, and self-esteem. These are powerful tools we're handing out to our primary students—tools that will serve them well throughout their school career. And they're a gift we give ourselves. Once your students have grown into independent writers, you'll find that they transfer the skills they've learned to other subjects during other times of the day. Everyone in your class will learn more because you have moved away from being traffic control officer to genuine teacher.

You'll know you've arrived when other adults come into your room and look around. "Where is the teacher?" they'll think. And then they'll see you seated amongst calm, productive students, entirely focused on the growth of a budding writer. I wish you joy in the transition.

Bibliography

Children's Books

Agee, Jon. 2005. *Terrific*. New York: Hyperion.
Cranky Eugene's luck changes when he meets a parrot on a deserted island. (organization, endings)

Agee, Jon, et al. 2006. *Why Did the Chicken Cross the Road?* New York: Dial.
Fourteen artists interpret the well-known riddle. (voice)

Ahlberg, Allan. 2008. *Previously*. New York: Walker.
Story told backward. (organization)

Banks, Kate. 2005. *The Great Blue House*. New York: Farrar, Straus and Giroux.
When its owners leave, a summer house comes alive with the sounds of a mouse nibbling crumbs in the fall, a cat taking shelter in the winter, and rain falling on the roof in the spring. (organization)

———. 2006. *Max's Words*. New York: Farrar, Straus and Giroux.
Max begins a word collection and discovers what he can do with it. (word choice)

Barrett, Judi. 1998. *Things That Are Most in the World*. New York: Atheneum.

Repeated sentence: The _____iest thing in the word is _____. (organization)

Barretta, Gene. 2006. *Now and Ben: The Modern Inventions of Benjamin Franklin*. New York: Holt.

Left-hand pages show inventions we use *now*; right-hand pages tell how *Ben* conceived and developed the idea. (organization)

Becker, Bonny. 2008. *A Visitor for Bear*. Somerville, MA: Candlewick.

Bear doesn't like visitors, but Mouse persists. (voice, fluency, refrain)

Bee, William. 2007. *The Train Goes . . . .* Somerville, MA: Candlewick.

Rollicking train story with the refrain, "and the train goes, Clickerty-click, clickerty-clack . . ." (fluency)

Bertrand, Lynne. 2005. *Granite Baby*. New York: Farrar, Straus and Giroux.

In tall-tale fashion, five mountain women cannot soothe the cries of a baby carved out of granite, but a little girl can. (organization, endings)

Billingsley, Franny. 2008. *Big Bad Bunny*. New York: Atheneum.

Who is Big Bad Bunny? A wee mouse named Baby Boo-boo. (voice)

Bolts, Maribeth. 2007. *Those Shoes*. Somerville, MA: Candlewick.

Jeremy wants the shoes that *everyone* at school is wearing. (organization, endings)

Bottner, Barbara. 1992. *Bootsie Barker Bites*. New York: Putnam.

A clever protagonist outwits Bootise the bully. (organization: pattern of three)

Brus, Deborah. 2001. *Book, Book, Book!* New York: Scholastic.

Bored, the animals go to the library, but only the hen can convey their needs. (onomatopoeia)

Bryant, Jen. 2008. *A River of Words: The Story of William Carlos Williams*. Grand Rapids, MI: Eerdmans.

Biography and poetry of William Carlos Williams. (beginnings, fluency, poetry)

Busse, Sarah Martin, and Jacqueline Briggs Martin. 2006. *Banjo Granny*. Boston: Houghton.

Granny's heart is set on seeing her new grandbaby, and she magically overcomes obstacles to do so. (beginnings, fluency, poetry)

Buzzeo, Toni. 2008. *The Library Doors*. Chicago: Upstart.
Introduces students to the library to the tune of "The Wheels on the Bus." (fluency)

Carle, Eric. 1991. *A House for Hermit Crab*. New York: Simon and Schuster.
After finding a new home, Hermit Crab asks other sea creatures to help him adorn his property. (quality details)

Cecil, Randy. 2007. *Gator*. Somerville, MA: Candlewick.
Gator, a seat on a carousel that's no longer in use, goes searching for a friend. (organization: pattern of three)

Chaconas, Dori. 2007. *Virginnie's Hat*. Somerville, MA: Candlewick.
Her wide-brimmed hat is blown up into a tree, and Virginnie is determined to get it down. (organization, pattern of three)

Charlip, Remi. 1994. *Fortunately*. New York: Simon and Schuster.
Alternates "fortunately" and "unfortunately" to tell story. (organization)

Chessa, Francesca. 2008. *Holly's Red Boots*. New York: Holiday House.
Holly and her cat search for her red boots. (everyday story, voice)

Church, Caroline Jayne. 2008. *Ping Pong Pig*. New York: Holiday House.
Ping Pong Pig wants to fly and makes big messes while trying. (organization, endings)

Cleary, Brian P. 2001. *To Root to Toot to Parachute: What Is a Verb?* Minneapolis: Carolrhoda.
A fun, lively look at verbs. (word choice)

Connor, Leslie. 2004. *Miss Bridie Chose a Shovel*. Boston: Houghton.
Story of Miss Bridie, who immigrates to America with shovel in hand. (organization, endings)

Cowley, Joy. 2005. *Chameleon, Chameleon*. New York: Scholastic.
The many moods (and colors) of chameleons. (voice)

Crimi, Carolyn. 2004. *Boris and Bella*. New York: Harcourt.
Bella Lagrossi is the messiest monster in Booville. Her neighbor, Boris Kleanitoff, is super clean. They both decide to have a Halloween party. (beginnings)

———. 2005. *Henry and the Buckaneer Bunnies*. Somerville, MA: Candlewick Press.
Henry does not want to be a pirate; he wants to read. (voice)

Cronin, Doreen. 2003. *Diary of a Worm*. New York: HarperCollins.
A young worm discovers, day by day, that there are some very good and some not-so-good things about being a worm in this great big world. Very funny! (point of view)

Cuyler, Margery. 1991. *That's Good! That's Bad!* New York: Henry Holt.

A boy floats away from the zoo on a balloon and encounters many adventures in the animal kingdom. This story alternates good and bad news. (organization)

Davies, Jacqueline. 2006. *The Night Is Singing.* New York: Dial.

All ready for bed, a little girl lingers, listening to the night's enchanting music—birds flying, branches creaking, the radiator sighing, the evening singing. (questions in text, sentence fluency)

———. 2007. *The House Takes a Vacation.* Tarrytown, NY: Marshall Cavendish.

A house takes its own vacation while its family is away on holiday. Clever puns. (organization, endings, word choice)

Davies, Nicola. 2005. *Ice Bear: In the Steps of the Polar Bear.* Somerville, MA: Candlewick.

Lyrical writing describes the awe-inspiring polar bear as it strives to survive in an age-old Arctic habitat threatened by global warming. (quality details)

Davis, Katie. 1998. *Who Hops?* New York: Harcourt.

A lively, silly read-aloud with a fabulous refrain. (fluency, refrain)

———. 2003. *Mabel the Tooth Fairy and How She Got Her Job.* New York: Harcourt.

Mabel the fairy neglects her teeth, but in the process of learning dental hygiene discovers her calling. (reader's theater available at www.katiedavis.com, fluency)

Diakite, Penda. 2006. *I Lost My Tooth in Africa.* New York: Scholastic.

A child loses a tooth in Mali. (everyday story)

Dipucchio, Kelly. 2005. *Mrs. McBloom, Clean Up Your Classroom.* New York: Hyperion.

Mrs. McBloom is retiring, and it's time to clean up her classroom! (quality details in text and illustrations)

Durango Julia. 2005. *Dream Hop.* New York: Simon and Schuster.

A boy skips from one harrowing adventure to another in his dreams. (organization, endings)

Eastman, P.D. 1960. *Are You My Mother?* New York: Random House.

Little Bird wants its mother. (organization)

Eliot, David. 2004. *And Here's to You.* Somerville, MA: Candlewick.

An ebullient celebration of animals—including people. (word choice)

English, Karen. 2004. *Speak to Me (And I Will Listen Between the Lines)*. New York: Farrar, Straus and Giroux.
Karen English imagines the thoughts of six third-grade children in one day and one classroom at an inner-city public school. (fluency, poetry)

Florian, Douglas. 1994. *Beast Feast*. New York: Harcourt.
Twenty-one original animal poems. (fluency, poetry)

Fox, Mem. 1985. *Wilfrid Gordon McDonald Partridge*. La Jolla, CA: Kane Miller.
A small boy tries to discover the meaning of "memory" so he can restore that of an elderly friend. (ideas, organization, endings)

Franco, Betsy. 2009. *A Curious Collection of Cats*. New York: Tricycle Press.
Concrete poems about cats, written in forms that include haiku, limerick, and free verse. (fluency, poetry)

Gantos, Jack. 1976. *Rotten Ralph*. Boston: Houghton.
Ralph really is a rotten cat, but Sarah loves him anyway. (organization, endings)

George, Lindsay Barrett. 2004. *Inside Mouse, Outside Mouse*. New York: HarperCollins.
Inside mouse and outside mouse mirror actions. Lots of frequently used words and prepositions. (onomatopoeia)

Giovanni, Nikki, ed. 2008. *Hip Hop Speaks to Children: A Celebration of Poetry with a Beat*. Naperville, IL: Sourcebooks Jabberwocky.
Poets included range from Langston Hughes and W.E.B. DuBois to Kanye West and Queen Latifah. (fluency, poetry)

Grey, Mini. 2005. *Traction Man Is Here!* New York: Knopf.
A child receives action figure in the mail. This story celebrates pretend play. (everyday story)

Hatkoff, Isabella, Craig Hatkoff, and Dr. Paula Kahumba. 2006. *Owen and Mzee: The True Story of a Remarkable Friendship*. New York: Scholastic.
The inspiring true story of two great friends: a baby hippo named Owen and a 130-year-old giant tortoise named Mzee. (found poetry)

Henkes, Kevin. 1991. *Chrysanthemum*. New York: Greenwillow Books.
Chrysanthemum wants a new name. (organization)

———. 2000. *Wemberly Worried*. New York: Greenwillow Books.
Wemberly, a shy white mouse, always feels nervous. (organization, pattern of three)

Hennessy, B.G. 2006. *The Boy Who Cried Wolf.* New York: Simon and Schuster.
A retelling of the classic tale with lovely repetition. (fluency, refrain)

Hort, Lenny. 2000. *The Seals on the Bus.* New York: Henry Holt.
Fun adaptation of "The Wheels on the Bus." (fluency)

Jacobson, Jennifer Richard. 1998. *A Net of Stars.* New York: Dial.
Etta wants to be brave enough to ride the Ferris wheel. (character names)

———. 1999. *Moon Sandwich Mom.* Joliet, IL: Albert Whitman.
Rafferty wants a new mother—a mother who is fun. (organization)

———. 2005. *Andy Shane and the Very Bossy Dolores Starbuckle.* Somerville, MA: Candlewick.
Andy is reluctant to go to school and engage with bossy Dolores. (quality details, word choice)

James, Simon. 1993. *The Wild Woods.* Somerville, MA: Candlewick.
While on a walk with Grandpa, Jess decided to keep a squirrel. (organization, pattern of three)

Janeczko, Paul B. 2005. *A Kick in the Head: An Everyday Guide to Poetic Forms.* Somerville, MA: Candlewick.
Lively anthology presenting twenty-nine different forms of poetry. (fluency, poetry)

Jenkins, Steve, and Robin Page. 2003. *What Do You Do with a Tail Like This?* Boston: Houghton Mifflin.
Explore the many amazing things animals can do with their ears, eyes, mouths, noses, feet, and tails. (organization)

———. 2005. *I See a Kookaburra! Discovering Animal Habitats Around the World.* New York: Houghton.
Animals organized by habitat. (organization)

———. 2006. *Move.* Boston: Houghton.
Animals are organized (in a chain) by the way they move. (organization)

———. 2007. *Dogs and Cats.* Boston, MA: Houghton.
This is a flip book: one half about cats, one half about dogs. (organization)

———. 2007. *Living Color.* Boston: Houghton.
Animals are organized by color. (organization)

———. 2008. *How Many Ways Can You Catch a Fly?* Boston: Houghton.
Facts are organized by prey. (organization)

Johnson, David A. 2006. *Snow Sounds: An Onomatopoeic Story.* Boston: Houghton.

Story is told in illustration and sound words. (onomatopoeia)

Juster, Norton. 2005. *The Hello, Goodbye Window.* New York: Scholastic.

A child visits her grandparents (quality details)

Keats, Ezra Jack. 1962. *The Snowy Day.* New York: Viking.

A child goes outside to play in the snow. (everyday story)

Kelly, Irene. 2007. *It's a Butterfly's Life.* New York: Holiday House.

A fascinating, delightfully designed, and at times whimsical look at butterflies. (quality details, nonfiction features.)

Knudson, Michelle. 2006. *Library Lion.* Somerville, MA: Candlewick.

A lion shows up at the library and is invited to stay—if he follows the rules. (organization, endings)

Krauss, Ruth. 1945. *The Carrot Seed.* New York: HarperCollins.

A little boy plants a carrot seed and helps it grow.

Kurtz, Jane. 2000. *River Friendly River Wild.* New York: Simon and Schuster.

Poems describing how a girl and her family—like Kurtz herself—survived the disastrous 1997 Red River flood in North Dakota. (fluency, poetry)

———. 2002. *Rain Romp.* New York: Greenwillow Books.

A rainy day makes one little girl feel mighty grouchy. (voice)

———. 2005 *Do Kangaroos Wear Seatbelts?* New York: Dutton.

A child questions safety measures while mom explains ways that all parents—humans and animals—keep their young safe. (organization, endings)

Kurtz, Jane, and Christopher Kurtz. 2002. *Water Hole Waiting.* New York: HarperCollins.

Monkey waits patiently at the water hole on the African Savannah. Gorgeous lyrical language, lively verbs. (word choice)

Lawson, JonArno. 2008. *Inside Out: Children's Poets Discuss Their Work.* New York: Walker.

A selection of verses from contemporary poets, and an explanation from each poet on how he or she developed the poem. (ideas, fluency, poetry)

Layne, Stephen L. 2007. *Love the Baby.* New York: Pelican.

One older bunny only *pretends* to love the baby—until he does! (show not tell emotions)

Lester, Helen. 1998. *Tacky the Penguin*. Boston: Houghton.
Tacky (with his quirky behaviors) saves his companions from the hunters. (organization, endings)

Lewis, J. Patrick. 2002. *Doodle Dandies: Poems That Take Shape*. New York: Atheneum.
Clever, playful volume that introduces children to "shape poetry." (fluency, word choice, poetry)

Long, Melinda. 2003. *How I Became a Pirate*. New York: Harcourt.
Jeremy Jacob joins Braid Beard and his pirate crew and finds out about pirate language, pirate manners, and other aspects of pirate life. (word choice)

Loomis, Christine. 2001. *Astro Bunnies*. New York: Putnam.
Bunnies go into outer space (poem to the rhythm of "Twinkle, Twinkle, Little Star"). (fluency)

Martin, Jacqueline Briggs. 2007. *Chicken Joy on Redbean Road: A Bayou Country Romp*. Boston: Houghton.
Miss Cleoma (a hen) sets out to find the fiddle player, Joe Bebee, so the blue-headed rooster will crow once again. (organization, endings, voice)

McCloskey, Robert. 1957. *Time of Wonder*. New York: Viking.
Excitement on a Maine island as a family packs to leave. (voice)

McMullen, Kate. 2002. *I Stink*. New York: HarperCollins.
The round of a garbage truck—told from the lively truck's point of view. (voice)

Moore, Libba. 1995. *My Mama Had a Dancing Heart*. New York: Scholastic.
The narrator recalls how she and her mother would welcome each season with dance. (organization, endings.)

Newman, Patricia. 2004. *Jingle the Brass*. New York: Farrar, Straus and Giroux.
Students use context clues to determine the meaning of "train talk." (word choice)

O'Connor, Jane. 2005. *Fancy Nancy*. New York: HarperCollins.
Nancy describes favorite words and their definitions. (word choice)

Page, Gail. 2006. *How to Be a Good Dog*. New York: Bloomsbury.
Cat trains dog to be good. (voice)

Parenteau, Shirley. 2007. *One Frog Sang*. Somerville, MA: Candlewick.
A counting book from ten to one featuring the many sounds of frogs. (onomatopoeia)

Perkins, Lynne Rae. 2003. *Snow Music*. New York: HarperCollins.
    Whispering, musical words describe winter scenes. (word choice,
    onomatopoeia)
———. 2007. *Pictures from Our Vacation*. New York: HarperCollins.
    Children go on a low-key vacation to a family farm. (quality
    details, everyday story)
Pilkey, Dav. 1996. *The Paper Boy*. New York: Scholastic.
    A boy and his dog rise early to deliver papers. (organization, endings)
Plourde, Lynn. 2002. *School Picture Day*. New York: Dutton.
    Josephina, a girl with curiosity and mechanical skill, saves the
    day. (organization, beginnings, fluency, refrain)
Pomerantz, Charlotte. 2006. *Thunderboom! Poems for Everyone*. New
    York: Front Street.
    Fifty-one verses with joyful sounds and wordplay. (fluency, word
    choice, poetry)
Prosek, James. 2004. *A Good Day's Fishing*. New York: Simon and
    Schuster.
    Describes a day of fishing with lots of specific fishing language.
    (word choice)
Pulver, Robin. 1994. *Mrs. Toggle's Beautiful Blue Shoe*. New York:
    Simon and Schuster.
    In a game of kickball, Mrs. Toggle kicks her shoe up into a tree.
    (organization, pattern of three)
Rathman, Peggy. 1995. *Officer Buckle and Gloria*. New York:
    Putnam.
    During Officer Buckle's safety presentations, Gloria steals the
    show. (onomatopoeia)
Regan, Dian Curtis. 2009. *Barnyard Slam*. New York: Holiday
    House.
    Unbeknownst to the farmer and his son, the barnyard animals
    participate in a lively poetry slam, hosted by Yo Mama Goose.
    (poetry)
Root, Phyllis 1996. *Aunt Nancy and Old Man Trouble*. Somerville,
    MA: Candlewick.
    Aunt Nancy out-tricks the trickster. (voice, onomatopoeia)
Rosenthal, Amy Kraus. 2005. *Little Pea*. New York: Chronicle.
    Little Pea wants to avoid candy. (organization)
Rowling, J.K. 1998. *Harry Potter and the Sorcerer's Stone*. New York:
    Scholastic.
    Models use of specific quality details. (quality details, word choice)

Rylant, Cynthia. 1985. *The Relatives Came*. New York: Scholastic.
Relatives come and share food and fun. (organization, beginnings, endings)

Sayer, April Pulley. 2005. *Stars Beneath Your Bed: The Surprising Story of Dust*. New York: Greenwillow Books.
Where does dust come from? A lyrical look: dust will never seem ordinary again. (quality details)

Schmidt, Karen. 1985. *The Gingerbread Man*. New York: Scholastic.
The traditional tale at a primary reading level. (fluency, repetition)

Schotter, Roni. 1999. *Nothing Happens on 90th Street*. New York: Scholastic.
Eva embellishes her story to make it more exciting. (word choice)

Seeger, Laura Vaccaro. 2007. *First the Egg*. New York: Roaring Brook.
Pattern: First the _____, then the _____. (organization)

Shannon, David. 1998. *No, David!* New York: Scholastic.
David moves from one misbehavior to another as his mother pleads, "No, David!" (focus)

Sidman, Joyce. 2005. *Song of the Water Boatman and Other Pond Poems*. Boston: Houghton.
This collection invites us to take a closer look at our hidden ponds and wetlands through science and poetry. (fluency, poetry, quality details)

———. 2006. *Butterfly Eyes and Other Secrets of the Meadow*. Boston: Houghton.
A stunning tour of the meadow through poetry and science. (fluency, poetry)

Stevenson, James. 2004. *No Laughing, No Smiling, No Giggling*. New York: Farrar, Straus and Giroux.
Interactive text (five stories) provides readers with rules: no giggling! (beginnings)

Stohner, Anu. 2005. *Brave Charlotte*. New York: Bloomsbury.
Charlotte is not a homebody, and her bravery helps her to save the day. (voice)

Sweet, Melissa. 2005. *Carmine: A Little More Red*. Boston: Houghton Mifflin.
While a little girl who loves red—and loves to dilly-dally—stops to paint a picture on the way to visit her grandmother, her dog Rufus meets a wolf and leads him directly to Granny's house.

Thompson, Lauren. 2005. *Mouse's First Snow*. New York: Simon and Schuster.

Mouse has a delightful romp in the snow. (word choice, onomatopoeia)

Timberlake, Amy. 2003. *The Dirty Cowboy*. New York: Farrar, Straus and Giroux.

Telling his faithful dog to make sure nobody touches his clothes but him, a cowboy jumps into a New Mexico river for a bath, not realizing that after the bath, his dog won't recognize him. (quality details)

Walker, Alice. 2006. *There Is a Flower at the Tip of My Nose Smelling Me*. New York: HarperCollins.

The five senses are celebrated in this volume of poetry. (fluency, poetry)

Ward, Cindy. 1997. *Cookie's Week*. New York: Putnam.

Organized by days of the week. (organization)

Wells, Rosemary. 2005. *McDuff Moves In*. New York: Hyperion.

One rainy night, a little white dog needed something to eat and a place to sleep. He went looking and found something he didn't expect—a home. (quality details)

Wheeler, Lisa. 2003. *Avalanche Annie: A Not-So-Tall Tale*. New York: Harcourt.

In this tall tale, Annie ropes an avalanche. (onomatopoeia)

———. 2006. *Mammoths on the Move*. New York: Harcourt.

A romping poem (with vivid verbs) about the migration of Wooly Mammoths. (word choice)

White, E.B. 1952. *Charlotte's Web*. New York: HarperCollins.

Wilbur the pig's life is saved by his friend Charlotte—a spider. (beginnings)

White, Linda Arms. 2005. *I Could Do That: Esther Morris Gets Women the Vote*. New York: Farrar, Straus and Giroux.

Story of the suffragette Esther Morris, who was the first woman to hold public office (even before women were granted the right to vote). (Quality details)

Wiesner, David. 2006. *Flotsam*. New York: Clarion.

A wordless picture book that tells the tale of an extraordinary camera and the undersea world it captures. (quality details, focus)

Willems, Mo. 2003. *Don't Let the Pigeon Drive the Bus!* New York: Hyperion.

Pigeon begs the reader to let him drive the bus while the driver is gone. (beginnings)

———. 2004. *Knuffle Bunny: A Cautionary Tale*. New York: Hyperion. Trixie leaves her bunny behind at the laundromat. (everyday, beginnings, organization)

Wood, Audrey. 1993. *King Bidgood's in the Bathtub*. New York: Scholastic.
King Bidgood's in the bathtub and he won't get out! Only the page knows what to do. (organization, endings)

———. 1994. *The Little Mouse, the Red Ripe Strawberry, and the Big Hungry Bear*. Swinden, UK: Child's Play.
Mouse keeps his strawberry from the hungry bear, until he decides to share. (onomatopoeia)

Yolen, Jane, and Andrew Fusek Peters, eds. 2007. *Here's a Little Poem: A Very First Book of Poetry*. Somerville, MA: Candlewick.
A collection of more than sixty poems by a wide range of talented writers, from Margaret Wise Brown to Gertrude Stein and Langston Hughes to A.A. Milne. (fluency, poetry)

Zimmerman, Andrea. 1999. *Trashy Town*. New York: HarperCollins.
Mr. Gilly cleans up Trashy Town in this fun, rollicking tale. (fluency, refrain)

Professional Books

Buzzeo, Toni. 2007. *Read! Perform! Learn! 2: 10 Reader's Theater Programs for Literacy Enhancement*. Janesville, WI: Upstart Books.

Calkins, Lucy. 1994. *The Art of Teaching Writing*. Portsmouth, NH: Heinemann.

Culham, Ruth. 2005. *6+1 Traits of Writing: The Complete Guide for the Primary Grades*. New York: Scholastic.

Freeman, Judy. 2007. *Once Upon a Time: Using Storytelling, Creative Drama, and Reader's Theater with Children in Grades PreK–6*. Westport, CT: Libraries Unlimited.

Giacobbe, Mary Ellen, and Martha Horn. 2008. *Talking, Drawing, Writing: Lessons for Our Youngest Writers*. Portland, ME: Stenhouse.

Jacobson, Jennifer Richard. 2007. *Graphic Organizers for the Overhead: Reading and Writing*. New York: Scholastic.

———. 2008. *Trait-Based Writing Graphic Organizers and Mini-Lessons: 20 Graphic Organizers with Mini-Lessons to Help Students Brainstorm, Organize Ideas, Draft, Revise, and Edit*. New York: Scholastic.

Jacobson, Jennifer Richard, and Dottie Raymer. 1999. *The Big Book of Reproducible Graphic Organizers.* New York: Scholastic.

Lane, Barry. 1999. *Reviser's Toolbox.* Shoreham, VT: Discover Writing Press.

Rog, Lori Jamison. 2007. *Marvelous Minilessons for Teaching Beginning Writing, K–3.* Newark, DE: International Reading Association.

Schaefer, Lola M. 2006. *Writing Lessons for the Overhead: Grades 2–3.* New York: Scholastic.

Skinner, B.F. 1964. *Science and Human Behavior.* New York: Free Press.

Spandel, Vicki. 2007. *Creating Young Writers: Using the Six Traits to Enrich Writing Process in Primary Classrooms.* 2nd ed. Boston: Allyn and Bacon.

Index

Page numbers followed by an *f* indicate figures.